Frost in Spring

AN ANTHOLOGY IN MEMORIAM

John H. Morgan, editor

Wyndham Hall Press

Bristol Banner Books

FROST IN SPRING

An Anthology in Memoriam

John H. Morgan, editor

Melinda Dunithan
Frost Anthology Coordinator

Anthony Oliver Norris
Associate Poetry Editor
Bristol Banner Books

Frost photo by permission
Dartmouth College Library

¶ Publishing since 1877, Bristol Banner Books is the poetry imprint of Wyndham Hall Press, Inc.

Library of Congress Catalog Card Number

89-40278

ISBN 1-55605-067-4

Printed in the United States of America

EDITORIAL NOTE

Twenty-five years seems such a short time but the void left by the death of Robert Frost persists in its magnitude. The grandeur of his simple language and the balance of sound embodied in his poetry seem ever to elude us in our enduring attempts to actualize the poetic.

This anthology has been gathered through the efforts of many poets and lovers of poetry. Wyndham Hall Press, Inc., and its poetry imprint, Bristol Banner Books, are to be once again congratulated for their relentless commitment to offering a creative forum for the aspiring poet to showcase new efforts through the memorial anthology series.

Wyndham Hall
Bristol, IN

J.H.M.
Winter, 1989

OUR LADY OF THE ROSE
Dedicated August 15, 1988

Divinely fraught is your loveliness
Our Lady of the Rose and rosary
As a rose in figure is your beauty
Our Lady clothed with sunlight
and with the zenith's azure
beneath your feet the crescent moon
shining silver of night's glamour
around your head a crown of stars
clustered to adorn your ardor
As a rose the kissing of your lips
to the rosy cheek, the crimsoned brow
As a rose your heart of feeling
enfolding fire through and through
but nothing speaks your splendor
or the nature of your wonder
as the simple action of your will
your 'So be it' beyond ponder
more powerful than atom's force
resound of galactic thunder
a rod to rule the serpent's weal
to break hell's gates asunder
the grace of love freely given
the glory of your grandeur.

Richard Adams

LAMENT ON AN UNREQUITED LOVE

The arrow failed, has missed its mark,
To heights and breadths we cannot see;
So I will shoot another - hark,
And so my quest shall be:
That searching the second shall find the first,
And rejoice with her in bliss;
From out of my heart, my love does burst,
Pledged in earnest with a kiss!

John P. Alexander

THE SEDUCER

His touch was not cold
As I thought it would be.
His quick breath's urgency
Did not seem old.

"Come with me," Death said.
How I wanted to go!
"Come with me, I will show
My fair, young dead."

I wept in despair
When he left, for I knew
His promises were true-
You await me there.

Helen Thomas Allison

THE POET

I have caught the shining splendour of a moment as it flies
to join the gathered ages of the past.
I have sent my eager thoughts to play beyond the farthest
skies,
and I've followed down the wake of every blast.

I have watched the white foam breaking where rapid water
flows,
seen the swift tides racing homewards free and strong.
I have held the dewy sweetness of a golden-hearted rose
and found its fragrance tangled in my song.

My soul has thrilled to loveliness with ecstasy of bliss
so intense that more than half of it is pain;
as when a woman trembles to her lover's tender kiss
and her shaken heart responds to him again.

So beauty takes my clumsy heart to sway and shatter it
with a multitude of unexplained desires,
that flare within as torches, whose hundred flames are lit
from the passion of her sacred altar-fires.

The mystery and music of the everlasting stars,
the meteor upon his fiery track,
the strange, magnetic holiness that shines in battle-scars,
and the broken Christ with scourge-marks on his back.

The Christ! the heart of beauty and the very heart of God!
his, his the fleeting image that I find,
and the word that leaps for utterance within this human clod,
is the shadow of a thought within his mind.

Rosemary Anne

AN OTHER OBSERVATION

A contemporary version of
"The Love Song of J. Alfred
Prufrock." --T.S. Eliot

When the morning is spread-eagled
let's go to the golden arches,
over the bumps and barricades;
let's go through clattering streets,
the screaming silence
of perfect lives in crackerbox suites
and somnambulent daze;
streets that never end like seasons
of football and baseball,
that lead to an undefined answer...
you know what it is. Why go out?
Let's stay home and pay our tributes.

Let no one come and stay
talking of another way.

The golden sphere that peeks over the edge,
the golden ball that bobs,
bounced into the corners of the room,
ignited curtains to sheets of flame,
took with it the morning dew;
through a cockroach crack it crept,
and seeing that it was dark all through,
impregnated their dreams while they slept.

Frank Anthony

KANSAS SPRING

April air bites at North winds as its
Spine-shivers shake budding branches.
Down the block redbuds fluff fuchsia
   smudging paint-pot blue skies
And forsythia blows lemon kisses
   at prim pink plums.

Scrubbed sidewalks hug scoop-edged lawns
And sentry overturned tyke-trikes dumped
   for last night's supper.

West of the wheatfields Bluebirds string Spring.
The Turtle-dove mourns the Season
And plumbs memories with its throb-song.

Bette Armstrong

WHO

Who interrupts me, with things better left unsaid?
Who rudely awakens me, when I've gone to bed?
Who tries to sell me something I don't want to buy,
and plagues me with surveys, of who, what, when where and
why?
Who says, "Good morning, and how are you today?"
The absolute clue, that a "sales-pitch" is on the way.
Who tells me I've just won a free carpet shampoo
and there's nothing more, I have to do?
Who says my name has been drawn to win a free prize--
anything from a watch to "flying the friendly skies?"
Who greets me with a cheery hello, as I drip from tub to
phone?
A computerized voice, in a MONOTONE!

Joan Auffart

FOR JED

The ocean shaped you like a shell
imprinted the spirals of your smile
forged the grooves of your walk
touched your iridescent underside.
I walk the beach alone
eyes focused out to sea
waves beckon me to where you lie
smooth and polished
buried treasure.

Michele Pauline Back

SUDDEN FLOWER

When God his soul does gently show
To me at some dark hour
A fragile grain of wisdom grows
From seed to sudden flower.

His startling light does swiftly part
Black sails of summer shower
And bathes the ocean of my heart
With his transcendent power.

When God his soul does hide from me
Like sun from winter's rain
My clouded heart strives to see
That sweetest flower again.

A wall of darkness sudden falls
Across the blackened bay
And the narrows of my heart
Knows not that brightest day.

When God his soul again does show
His unrelenting power
My violent heart does quick unfold:
A small, eternal flower.

A. Lacy Baldy

YOUR SERVANT THE WIND

Holy Lord, Your Servant the Wind blows softly by me each day,
And his touch speaks of the love You pour out in so many ways.
With his help, the flowers bow low in adoration and prayer.
He lifts and carries the birds' joyful chorus for all to hear and share.

Holy Lord, Your Servant the Wind calls to me in the night.
He tells me about the One Creator, the God of Power and Might.
He causes the tops of the trees to dance while the leaves join in to sing.
Together, they offer a hymn of praise to You, Almighty King.

Holy Lord, Your Servant the Wind tells out Your glory abroad.
In roaring swells and in gentle breezes, he proclaims that You are God!
Faithfully, in trust he moves, obedient to Your commands.
At the sound of Your voice, he is calm and still, an instrument in Your hands.

Holy Lord, Your Servant the Wind reminds me of all that I am...
Your creation, the child You love, a part of Your perfect plan.
Father of All, may I do as much to make You known to all men!
May my voice and touch tell others of You, just like Your Servant the Wind.

Nancy Bartlett

LIFE

Can it be always when day is done
There is a feeling that life's been won?
Myriads of memories daily pass by;
When the day's over sometimes I cry.
Oh what a feeling life is so deep,
A fulfilled promise that one must keep.
Life is in a day; quickly it may pass
With the sun's ray and a solemn mass.
Yet as sun goes down around the whole earth
Man and beast know how much life is worth!

Merle Beckwith

I AM MAN

This my time of trial, of need,
Do I succumb to lust and greed?

May God endow me with the power
To make of this my shining hour?

Temptation now in many forms,
Lust for power, wealth, a woman warm,

May I be guided by the cross?
God give me strength that I may not be lost,

Lost in the wilderness of lust and greed,
I've been tempted, I've felt the need

For wealth, power, a woman warm,
God help me build a shelter against the storm

Created by man's natural inborn state,
I need Thy help to fight temptations great,

I need Thy help that I may see
the only way that's right for me,

The only door to heavens' gate,
I need thy help, God, I am man in natural state.

George E. Bell

APART

You were dear to me;
though to you it meant but little.
Our lives ran separate but parallel.
Your wounds I felt; your risks
left me vulnerable.
Broken bonds, tears,
    achievements, hopes and dreams
    were yours and mine until
    one day the window through which
        I saw you
        seemed dark
        and reflected the image
        of me alone.

Mary A. Bell

UNIVERSITY AVENUE

Along this threadbare carpet
leading to the throne of higher learning
we pass through darkness
past the burned-out hotel
where transients lost a kind of home,
past grilled fronts, deceptively ornamental,
and the dark shapes of men drowning in shadows
for the quick fix. Here, too, the bag ladies
scratching for an innocent place to sleep;
above them the quick-fix leveration graffiti.

Green, uncrowded places call,
and I would leave the memory of this blight.

So once I banished places of my youth
which, sea changed, nestle yet within me,
refusing to be turned out.
Sores heal, scabs wear away to a rosy pink,
memory likes the color green.
Even the deprived have their stories, told with animation,
for when the lesser is all we've known,
we settle for that. And the eye that registers the dark
is the same that looks for blossoms in a golden light,
and finds them in the most unlikely place.

Will I look back to this pedestrian land
and see the horses prancing?

Dorothy V. Benson

TOUCH

People all around people in frustration
life goes on in such a beautiful way.

Kindness coming from within kindness coming
from without feel the air and find the
helping hand.

Hear the laughter and the tears with each other
we move along. Someone there if you look
always help if you search.

Let the anger disappear and bring the peace
with each helpful smile. So many people
passing along so many faces searching for peace.

Don't drown in a dream live the dream and see
reality, we go on with our lives making it
through the blaze. Touch each other let the
other touch you, smile gently and life gets
better.

Isabelle Miranda Bento

FLICKERING CANDLE

Well, Thomas, are you getting the rest
you deserve after poems have met the test?

Good grief, has it been this long since we met
at that hotel when we both were deeply in debt?

Your name is constantly on the tips of tongues.
Even of those standing on Painters' ladder rungs.

The candle of Hope flickers when we arrive there
in a crowded city smelling with polluted air.

Poets today say land is getting better now.
I don't know, Thomas, pastures are without cow.

Jack Bernier

"EMPIRICALLY"

Empirically this is meant
    not as an excuse
        only stating facts.

It is perfectly understandable
    why one would turn to drugs.

Even evolutionary true
    that nature has provided the means
        of raising consciousness
            by chemoreceptor stimulus.

To be forewarned is to be forearmed
    so the saying goes
        the dangers are intense.

Evolution now demands
    altered states of consciousness.

Peer pressures and the likes
    insecurities too
        not are they
            the seekers of the light.

Paradoxically, once the way is known
    be that chemicals booze and such
        the next stage to reach
            is to actualize altered states
                without dependences of any kind.

Then feel no shame
    having been human enough
        to be helped "EMPIRICALLY"

David M. Bittlingmeier

SPRING IN APPALACHIA

Fields are being coaxed to green.
Clay lies coppery on the river banks
And white birches are peeling brown.

The hills are still a charcoal study,
But near the thicket's edge
Green tendrils wrap and circle
Urging the trees to wake from their sleep.

Water seeps from the hills
Polishing white the stones.
Streams loll with indecision.

Yellow moss nurtures on limbs
Hewn by the winter storms.
Flying saws shape lean the lumber.

Boys play by the creek with new found freedom
Unshackled from the bundlings of winter
Savoring the awakening land.

Hoe and plow are worked again
With hope, fear and determination.
Spring can be as ruthless as a mountain lion
Stalking her prey on padded tread
Or as carefree as the mutterings of a child at play.

Jean L. Blagg

YOUR DAY

It is beautiful ... it is new
It is a time for you
In which to partake.

Accept it, enjoy it, anticipate
    new experiences
        new inspirations
            new wisdom
                a
                  n
                    d
                      new blessings.

It will not come to you again,
It has not been with you before,
So as it wanes

Softly close the door
    with gratitude
        with understanding
            with love
                a
                  n
                    d
                      with a prayer.

Dorothy Cowley Blake

THE MUSIC OF RAIN

on a gray overcast day,
  the steady falling rain
    hitting windows and streets
      washing and cleansing
music playing on the radio:
  birds singing all day
some is melody;
  some is noise.
honking car horns
  in heavy city traffic,
    congesting the walk.
Nature's music and sounds
  obscured by man's noise.
steady falling rain,
  falling rain,
    waterfalls,
      ocean tides,
        water fountains,
listening
  to the steady
    beat and rhythm
watching
  with fascination
    as waves break over rocks.

Eve J. Blohm

THE WINDS OF HEAVEN

My body is a temple--
    not of stones and mortar,
but of substance much
    more permanent. It is
a vessel shaped to fit
    Your needs. But...
It stood unoccupied
    for many years...and filled
with much debris and
    many weeds.
When I at last unlocked
    the door, ... before
twas fit for You to dwell,
    You sent a host of angels in
to cleanse and purify
    each room. And then ...
You opened all the
    windows wide,
and let the winds of heaven
    blow inside.

Mary Hattan Bogart

LIFE WENT ON

I planted a tree for someone to climb
Somebody chopped it down
But life went on.

I built a house for someone to live in
Somebody tore it down
But life went on.

I lit a fire for someone to keep warm by
Somebody put it out
But life went on.

I wrote a poem for someone to read
Somebody read it
So I planted another tree, built
another house, and lit another fire

Life went on.

Katrina Boguski

JORGE LUIS BORGES

A poet is a poet is a man
A creature of the darkness and the night
Who sees through dark of darkest nightfall darkness
Without, within, wherever is the light
Then seeing; stumbles, tumbles, follows, races after
To find it, catch it, hold it 'til it goes
To seek, inspect, divine light's truth in snatches
Knowing as he holds it, it will go
Leaving him in darkness as before
To suffer once again black bath of agony
As he waits, and waits, and waits, and waits still more
Always on his knees while even standing
Heart bowed and bended to the floor
Eyes that blink and peer through endless darkness
Beholding nothing; seeing so much more.

Thomas Arthur Bonebrake
(died June 10, 1987)

WALKING

I thought of how my walk has been;
    the agony I've shared with Him.
I thought of how He's come to me
    when I've been down on bended knee.
A brother or sister caring for me -
    lifting their light so I could see -
That he was there and hadn't gone -
    and helped him then, as I was "born."

So, don't despair, the Lord is there
    in the midst of pain and care.
He picks you up and hugs you tight,
    and takes away the fear and fright.
He comes in deepest stress and woe
    to those who suffer here "below."
He waits for all to come and stay
    near to his wounded side today.

Today's the day and not the next
    for all the worried and perplexed.
He is the answer tried and true
    down through the ages waiting for you.

Evelyn H. Bostick

EVE

Do not take Eve for granted: I, too, am she
Returned, inscrutable Guardian of this place,
Now in my thicket hiding from your face
Doomed and rehearsing what my lines must be.
It was no serpent that persuaded me
Out of your avenues reserved for grace;
I had no quarrel with the special case
Settled apart for your forbidden tree.
That fruit you mentioned already on the ground
I saw, windfallen, when in the early day
I happened past; I heard its contacting sound
And thought with proper care and good assay
What pity such a thing should go to waste.
I did not eat the fruit: I did but taste.

Beverly Boyd

GRAYLOCK

From what violent eruptions were you born?
Majestic, defiant, you answer me -
"I was here before this valley -
Before civilizations, created in havoc.
Water coursing down my face.
Snows avalanching.
I change and not change.
Trees dare to grow in my crevices.
I do not belong to man
I am God's mountain
Eternal as He."
I reply - 'I know.
Before we were - you were.
When we are no more - you will be.
Eons of sunshine, star and moonlight,
Clouds playing in your peaks
Cast shadows and change your moods.
Winter on winter -
Spring and summer in turn -
Snows melting - torrents of rain;
Rocks tumbling down.
But there you stand
impregnable, inscruitible.

Helen Beach Boyle

PATIENTS

Faucets turn softly
on new stems
like roses to the sun

Bath drains quickly
sweetly
to the gurgle and bubble
of unobstructed waste

A friendly snake
probes curve and coil of copper pipe
intestines large and small

A wounded commode
has its trap removed

Plumbers
dear creatures
perform bypasses and transplants
mercifully

Libby Brahms

THE GREATEST IS LOVE

Make my love transparent,
crystal - clear and lucid,
all colors convergent
prism's sunburst - vivid

RED - affection of youth
sometimes a noisy gong
arrogant, rude, uncouth
sings a beloved song.

YELLOW - the sunshine years
warmth nurturing the child
patience that bears all things
loving the juvenile.

BLUE - through the glass darkly
a challenge - sickness, strife
now childish ways set free
enjoys a caring life.

B. J. Bramhall

MY MICHIGAN

Let me close my eyes and
Go back through the years
To the days of my childhood,
Its joys and its tears.

Let me roam all alone
Through the Michigan wood,
Know a child's wondrous love
Of all that is good.

Let me hold in my hands
The flowers and fern,
And see once again
Lake Michigan churn.

Let me stand on the top
Of the sand dunes so high,
Look down through the Pine trees
Where The Black River lies.

Let me feel once again the wintry air
And the new falling snow on my face.
I long to see the icebergs on the lake
My old home, my dear friends, my birthplace.

Then let me climb in the Spring
Through the hill's grassy dew,
Where lilies of the valley and
Luxuriant wildflowers grew.

Yes, let me feel once again
The nearness to God,
That I knew as a child
On Michigan's sod.

Beverly Brown

THE SECOND TRYST

The vocabulary of parting
    stings my tongue
dismembered letters cut my days
    to sighs,
fragments of trysts remain, pale souvenirs--
    remnants of shattered consonants of pride
whose sunsets flamed the skies like ripened plums
    plucked from a broken branch of Paradise.

Let me learn newer words that turn to green
    a crocus stream of sounds to herald Spring
        a lexicon of loveliness caught in rhyme
to paragraph the lark's brief morning phrase.
    Let me live lines of Southwind poetry
    whose hidden beauty has a sonnet's sweep
a metered strength that will be mine to keep
    triumphant, as I search the ocean skies;
        recapturing the essence of a spell
            irrevocably my own, not fantasy,
            an intimation of another world
    whose language is a lyric meant for me.

Helen T. Brown

A THEME TO LIVE BY

Events which daily pass us by
As well as all the things we try,
Can make our lives so very full,
Or on the other hand, quite dull.
It all depends on what we do
And how we treat those people who
May cross our path from day to day,
No matter what they do or say.

FOR:--

We all should know there is no way
To think just of ourselves each day.
Our Lord has taught us we should care
And with our neighbors always share
The good things that we get from God
Without a need for gentle prod.
For everyone's our family
If we accept them gratefully.

Harrison Wilder Bullard

GOODNIGHT SWEETHEART

Goodnight sweetheart, until a new tomorrow
    Dawns fair, and bright -
Upon our brand new day.
Until we see the rossette hues of morning.
Renew our love, and you sweetheart
    belong to me.

Goodnight sweetheart, the earth is hushed and
    The nightingale has ceased silent
    Its song above.
And you my darling, when you wake tomorrow
Will see fulfillment of our new found love.

Goodnight sweetheart.
    If sorrow comes between us.
Together we will face what'ere may come.
    Though tears shall flow -
    if we should have to part dear.
We'll meet in purest sunshine
    up above.

Edith Burrage

THEY SAY, YOU KNOW WHAT? YOU KNOW?
(a Late 20th Century Ditty)

They say cantilevers revolutionized architecture, they say
  A house is not a home without a tax, they say.
My mare is not a horse but computerized breeding's finest
  product, if what I've heard is true.
  More the pity, they say.
Routine breeds force of habit, an integrated personality
  perhaps? you know.

They say, a station break fractures your soap,
  Supposedly supporting a serial segment, they say.
Some entertainment strengthens leisure, grants it grace, they
  say.
I'd shy away from that if I were you, you know.

They say it's half baked ideas that fertilize
  the entire planet, they say.
If exercise extends existence, they say, your average
  depends more upon vertical options, not so permanently
  perpendicular as they thought, they say, you know.

You know, you know, You know what?
It's 10 o'clock and we all know where your children are,
  you know.
What do you know about that?
Skinner relates the world's always been some sort of ballooning
  conditioned reflex complex, you know.
  You just think you think, you know.
So much more to control you with, my dear, they say.

Bob Bush

FOR VALERIE

"There is sunshine in the darkness",
I read yesterday.
"God is ever-present when He seems
So far away".

Love is always constant
When you feel it not.
Joy, abundant, overflowing,
Erases every blot.

Jodi Sloan Cahill

I TOSS THE BALL HIGH, ABOVE MY HEAD

Sun-faded and worn
Rain-dirty and broken.
I toss the ball, high above my head.

My being longs, heavenwardly.
And is there.
Until I grasp the falling ball in my hand.

I toss the ball high above my head.

Jane W. Campbell

ALONE

The injured heart is a beast at bay,
Fronted by a spitting, snarling antagonist.

So, like a cat, I stalk away
To lick my wounds in private
And hide beneath the bramble bush.

As dusk steals across the land,
From my dark hiding place
Stealthily I creep forward
And sniff the curdling milk
    in saucer left behind,
And prowl about on padded feet
That leave neither sound nor trace.

Then back I slink to the bramble bush,
And wary, wait and watch,
With green eyes glowing in the dark;
But no one comes or calls.

Weary at last, I curl myself into a ball,
To sleep--alone and cold.

Ruth Campbell-Tuomi

THE FALL

It was not the unity but the separation,
Not the separation but the relationship,
Not the relationship but the need

That Creation broke,
The Son bled
And Spirit spoke:

What was many is one
What was dead is alive
What was absent is present

In a mind where unity needs separation,
Where separation needs unity,
And need is the beginning and end of it all.

Christopher Carlisle

THE FROG POND

Trees claw the sky
With naked limbs
As if the moon
Might save them from
Drowning behind
The landfill

Luna caught by
The mire's surface
Shines clearer
than its twin above.

Yvonne Carpenter

KEEPERS OF THE MYSTERY

There's something in a window
that suits a cat
    surveyor of a kingdom
    ruler and judge of all it views

In not so familiar
suburban night
    silent stark silhouettes
    formed of ebony and shadow
    cut and framed like idols
        defending catacombs
    demand worship
poised, waiting

William A. Carter

BOSTON IVY

Lord,
your glorious Boston ivy
weaves its threads around my house
in endless twists of tendril curls,
dappling the ugly dark
and pocked brown
of ancient asbestos
into an undulating gown
of sparkling green.

O God!
would that I, too,
might sprout yellowpink buds
that burgeon into verdant webs,
robing me
in a Boston ivy thicket
where asbestos dies in the night
and vine leaves glisten
in a new morning sun.

Anthony Chiarilli

WHO SAYS, "NOT DIED IN VAIN"?

With uncertain (but respectful) fury,
We endured the open grave,
The cold, gray coffin now embracing him
Who had but few days past embraced the bullet.
"He has given all to save his country."
So they said of him who faced the sudden winter
Of his flesh--this boy, this barely-more-than-child.
Dark death had settled on his eyes,
Concealing all the half-truths, all the lies.

What did he, in childhood, know of wars?
Of politics? Of international manipulations?
These are not the games of children. WHO COULD CARE?
Remove him from the hovel of his poverty,
And let him fight. By all means, let him share
With others crying out to life: "KEEP ME! KEEP ME!"
And if the cry is useless--what of that?
(A soldier should die young, before the loss of faith.)
And if some die to never walk again
Among the lilacs and the roses, let them lie.

But by whatever gods exist on high,
A time will come when some will have to walk
In silence, listening (in guilt)
To hear the world's last anguished cry--
The high, thin song of all the tortured meek.
(The way the soul would sound, if it could speak.)

J. A. Christensen

SNOW BULLETIN

We wake to the great goose feather fall
giving a decent burial to MacDonald
containers, dog turds -- all unsightly
residues of man and beast. Elk hound,
Eskimo spitz trot with thrilled feet,
winter's madness in them. Headlighted
cars inch forward as though chained
together. Out back, rose smoke
hovers, street lamps struggle to pierce
it; and that sound, that aurora borealis
whisper, is the snow's voice, speaking.

Shirley G. Cochrane

TO VIRGINIA

Your snail curled in the corner, in the
side of imagination,
Worming its way into words and boring
through the concrete of our perceptions,
Eeling its slender persuasions toward the inner
darkness, peeling the dark core away.
You've seen us, desperate swimmers, gliding up from the
mud, lodged in the nets,
Fright and fight gone, sentient of the extremities
of nature and the limitless
possibilities for pain.

Pat Colosi

TOMORROW'S NEWS

Every morning for twenty years, the man
across the street has come out of his house
at six A.M., each morning, picked up the news
paper, unfolded it, glimpsed headlines as he
reentered the house, slammed the door loudly behind
him. I watched this morning over three cups
of coffee, two more than I usually drink.
By lunch the paper still lay on the walk
like a limp white puppy. I called at two
o'clock in the afternoon. The phone growled
into my ear a dozen times or more.

No one answered.

We have never been what you might call friends,
just holler across the street from time to time:
comments on the weather or the ball game.
By 6 P.M. a premonition began
to crawl icily through me. I walked slowly
across the street and pushed open the door.

He will be tomorrow's news.

Louise Wilkerson Conn

SUMMER VISITORS

The world is a-quiver with joy today!
Bird and butterfly swoop or flutter.
Sun glinting off iridescent wings,
They search for insects, dip from the flowers,
Tasting the bounty nature brings.
Alive to the wonders of this shining hour.

How far did they fly in the last few days?
On their long migration from hotter climes?
Where they bask in the warmth of a friendlier sun.
While winter held us in her frigid grip.
'Til they felt the compulsion of nature's call,
And eagerly started their arduous trip!

I wonder at how such fragile wings,
Could span the vast uncharted miles.
Return to the homeland from whence they came.
To nest in our trees, raise their young.
Brighten our summer with beauty and song.
In autumn they'll leave to follow the sun!!

Patti Cordell

SILENT OAK TREES

When Family's Settled on Strange Land so
Long Ago
Planted Oak Trees here and there-finding
Such Peace

They grew Strong Defying Winds that Howled
All Hours
The Blossoms grew into Full Bloom like
Happy Flowers

The Wise Thrush Sings on Branches High
Sending Rapture

Lovers Carved their Names-Vowing to Always
Be True

Golden History Lingers and the Old Trees
Remember Well
Souls of Settlers Dead and Long Gone
at Rest
Leaving Their Spirit Lingering in the Woods
to Protect

Bidding Farewell to wait until given Happy
Eternal Life!

Hazel Corey

ADAM IN EXILE -- THE FIRST NOVEMBER

Tell the stringleg and the hundredfoot
How the niggling tick of fear
Disrupts the moment's idleness.

Tell the cloud. Tell soot
And clotted clay how waterdroplets clear
As crystalglinting gather to press

A string of mockery through the brow
Each time the dawn comes crossed with dew
Or twilight with a shower. Bark

To the fox our hunger. Hoof the cow
After ten days' rain in the mire. Strew
The hay of our loss in the dark.

Tell the thicket that patience we need to learn
Is stoned under moss, soiled too deep below fern.
It is cold. The smoke of our breath is too stern:
We cannot return to the garden or we burn.

Tony Cosier

OMNIPOTENT

Dry lightning spawned
    infernos
Nature consumed by nature.
Brands upon the mountainside
The Almighty staked His claim.

Skeletal trees and dawn
    stood
Strangely still.
Golden light dispelled the gloom
In the shadow if the valley
White morning glories bloomed.

Anne L. Cowley

LIFE'S PANORAMA

A life a noble creed can be;
Its panorama of events
From birth unto eternity
A devotee to circumstance...
To joy, to sorrow; to gain or loss,
To love, to hate; to take or give,
Frequently denied a choice
While seeking plateaus on which to live;
High in the eyes of men to be,
But in the Plan of God, much more...
Above the worldly plenary
Aloft as an eagle a life could soar.

Phyllis Crago

THE HEART MUST COME TO WINTER

And the berries shall ripen
among the thorns, at the meadows edge
out of reach of tender hands.

There is no tumor growing.

There is again the crocus
and the mocking bird -
and there, a violet blooms.

The caprice of wild running waters
drenched the willows
and summer tasted sweet.

There is no sun forever.

Yellow leaves rustle autumn
and golden rod has faded
and the bob-white
intent on flooding his call
with dawn and dusk -
until the valley orchards
release sweet apples -
and journeys never come to an end
and night has come with import
to the center of breath.

No cage can hold
all the orioles -
the heart must come to winter.

Emma Crobaugh

THE GREAT MYSTERY

I descended into your mists from my castle in the air
to see what I could find to await me there
I saw many things that were strange but true
I did many things that I no longer do
I left everything behind that had bin important to me
to search for peace and love and to be happy and free
But what seemed to be was not to be the thing I was lookin
for
But eventually I found it on a quite unexpected shore
Now to-day if I try to tell you exactly what it is I found
You would say that I'm crazy and that my mind is unsound
But I know that it's real. It's tested and true
in many hard times it's brought me thru
So what to me is quite crystal clear
has been muddied thru ages of lies and fear
So that the truth for you remains hidden and covered
Because you can't see the great truth I've discovered
But all thru the ages anyone can see
if they really want to the great mystery

Karla Cummins

ONLY SHADOWS

Moon-days of summer,
and the night's blind lament:
only wasted crosses
upon the rounded gestures
of hills.
In the distance,
the echo of stars
as we begin again our slow ascent
from midnight's broken need.
The labyrinths in our eyes,
the moisture beneath our shadows,
receive memory's spiral:
how many footsteps in a lifetime?
The flight of sparrows flutters
with musty myths,
while the breeze lifts up
the smell of pines and birches,
and a black-green darkness
lies rotting on the humid ground.

Nirmal Dass

PATTERNS

"Why should the aged eagle stretch its wings?" T.S. Eliot

Above us, something twists the sky
in patterns that it must have learned
the first day it began to fly.

We look up expecting a magpie
or gull, city birds who turn
up in turgid air and urban sky.

We call in an expert watcher, my
friend who catalogues gulls, terns,
everything that lifts the eye.

He says it is a predator but why
it's here he can't discern,
above us twisting up the sky

far from its usual prey, its cry
as silent as its wings that churn
the city air it claims to fly.

Let thunder roar, let lightning burn.
The aged eagle twisting the sky
seeks witnesses who will confirm
its patterns, its license to fly.

Diana Der-Hovanessian

TO A FRIEND

I suppose the story is your own,
though a page from your book
forces me to plagiarize the outcome.
I ran swiftly to property that
held a deep well, drilled hard;
suddenly, there was water flowing.
I caught a perfect fish -- answers
are not as easy as that, usually.

When needed the water walks by itself,
and I, upon it, touch each hand
that lends a knowing.
Hurrah! Together we write a complete story.
Though I cheated on my paper,
the threads of wood will last, will
keep on pushing page after page.
And I? I will feed my fish to
keep it growing.

Frances Desloge

SATISFIED

The LOVE, I long for ----- is right here
As I listen ----- with the inner ear.
Here none deceive ----- nor can deceive
As from sense to Soul receive.

Here LOVE unfolds one's way ---
Ageless, flawless, limitless day.
Radiancy drawn by Perfect MIND.
In His true Presence, I find,
Beauty and Truth eternally are
Transforming my scar to a radiant star!!

Alicia Devereaux

DELTREAN'S FLIGHT

Little one, you had everything on a silver platter
But for you it didn't matter
Yes, fate took you by the hand
And led you down a road no one can understand

You were born for mission to travel to the stars
Led by the crying guitars
Unwilling to touch the ground
You are in love with the new atmospheres you have found

Occultation leaves you free to wander the heavens
Melting the years by sevens
You move with trepidation
Fleeing to the Nebula seeking consultation

Deltrean
Tell me girl, what do you hear?
Is it your world that you fear?
Oh, what makes you fly away?
Is it the dawn of each new day?
Tell me girl

Looking into other's eyes, peacefully like a dove
You orbit round those who love
And Momma cries late at night
Everytime she thinks of her baby Deltrean's flight.

Colleen Devlin

THE BUS SIGHED

The bus was grimy
and age oozed
from the seats.
It seemed to sigh
each time another kid
got on.
We always stopped at
this one house
to pick up a girl
that didn't look
so good.
A lot of the big kids
made fun of her.
She just couldn't
meet their standards.
She would sit there
and sigh,
just like the bus.

Wayne Dowdy

SPLINTERS

Reeling thoughts fleet,
Like fingers racing down dark banisters,
Yearning for light;
Breathy, cloud-dappled feelings are crazy
With swelling scarlet maizes.
Deep, spreading hands carry me,
Swiftly dropping me beyond
Liquid daisy fields;

I escape,
As ambling summer days fade away,
Like dreams.

Dainne Drilcok

DAILY OFFICE: LITTLE GIDDING

In the great chamber of amber light,
wainscoating and brass
ladies first to assemble at night's
break, ready in black dress

and veils, the saintly company,
capes against November chill,
skirts shuffling and yard upon
yard of cloth fanning round until

hall becomes a printed
broadside of black and white.
Boys and men, indented
in line, the master in tight

board and gown, lads in collarless
shirts and bloomers; godly Deacon
in surplice and hood,
fellow of Clare, Cambridge colors.

In seemly procession across
dewy Huntingdonshire fields
in fair greenery,
adorned by low clouds.

Manor house in the morning sun,
cattle running to their own
orisons, the congregation
filing through meadows of briars,

thistles, and tall grass, nearer
each step the holy chapel,
to sing matins in beauty
and order, to pray and kneel

on tapestries of art and chant
from cloth-of-gold, where
the eagle and crowned font
light darkened oakwood walls

With tapers the first lessons
instruct the day, punctuation
of blessings.

In slight interruption
of charitable sleep, holy family
and holy friends hidden from the world
by angels of the shire --

Still, quiet, blessed,
with tapers the first lessons
instruct the day,
a punctuation of blessing.

Travis DuPriest

YOU CAN

Skip the waves; tear the night;
Follow geese along their flight;
Or, catch the purple dawning
When it's born.

Spin the song; knit the tale;
Hit the hammer with the nail;
Lead the marchers with a
Buttered horn.

Fly the moon; dance the wind;
Tell the storm when to end;
Or, dare to seek the grail
In face of scorn.

Be President; hike the wages;
Act the drama of the ages;
(But, ease the hearts of those
Who, loving, mourn?)

Kitty Beasley Edwards

COME IN CHRIST'S NAME

With great expectation
They entered the door;
A hunger was felt
To know Jesus once more.

Their lives were not easy
With trials that came,
But hope gave them courage
To come in Christ's Name.

The years had brought sadness,
But hope brought a light
To shine through the darkness
As love came in sight.

The past was now over,
New life was in view;
They prayed for the Spirit
To show what to do.

Instead of sad faces
A joy was now seen.
Forgiveness from Jesus
Had washed their souls clean.

The Family gives welcome
To sinners as friends
As the Spirit with Love
On God's people descends.

Frances C. Emmons

WHY CAN'T I WRITE A BLOODY POEM?

Why can't I write a bloody poem?
I've got the thoughts inside.
But when I go to write them down
They run away and hide.
The words just will not come to me
To say the things I feel,
And when I get a little start,
It loses its appeal.
It's really rather difficult
To try to paint with words.
My messianic monologues
Can really sound absurd.
The themes are always sicky-sweet
Or frought with bitter pain
Or angry vicious homilies
Or moons that wax and wane.
They're so extreme they go too far
And overstate the theme,
Or Fassbinder would call them weird
Like Andy Warhol's dream.
I wish that I could speak to you
And move you with my pen,
But now I guess I'll have to quit
And later try again.

Mary Louise Firth

TIME

Stillness of time
passes without echo ...
For only man, not time, records.

Time is untouched by rain.
Unmindful of sun -- passing by
tumult of war and dirge of death.

Time can't be held in your hands
... It holds you in its grasp.

Winnie E. Fitzpatrick

STREET PEOPLE

They're just like one of us
But fate has changed the course
With a little bit of bad luck
Now just a victim of the system
Trying to live and survive
The world has turned upside down for them
And now they're washed up in the tide
Now they follow the pattern of wind
Cause they got no place to be
You see them on the sidewalks
Living so dangerously
The sub-ways and the parks
Are now they're home
And in the day-time
They just wander and roam
It could happen to anybody
Yes, it could happen to you and me
Cause the high-price of living
Is not what it use to be!

Gary W. Fort

INSPIRATION

Always there's something small
that wants its life
swings green and squiggling
in the crucial air
drops plumb like
from a blade of grass
scuttles dashes from my path

Always there's some small way to care
I think of Dr. Schweitzer:
Knowing lights of summer nights
invite the moths to die
he read by day.

Alessa Foster

ULTIMATUM: SUBSTANTIALITY

Your initials may be AM
But does that make you King
  Arthur
My initials say empty
But does that mean

  I lack

The quintessential me?
You're Wordsworth!
This is neither a breastplate

  nor a bib

 Unless you are

  King

  Arthur

Meg Taney Founds

REQUIEM FOR MYSELF

Isak Dinesen once said
A sleeping cat could make
Of any room a place
Of peace and comfort

I hope,
When I am dead,
Someone will say of me,

"A cat has left the room."

Hannah Fox

MANAGERIAL GRIDLOCK

All corporate charts show slots
for lots of managers,
in truth, well-paid mail clerks
impaled on piles of rules
and other limitations--
in imitation of ants.

While munching snacks at desks
they sift their memo stacks
and keep staff meetings brief,
yet for the Chief, far longer;
no room in which to think:
Bureaucracy in bloom!

Richard Franklin

THE LAST PILOT

King of the air, master of the skies
My throne a silvery jet
Pulsing with power, it flies.

My crown, reflection of sunlight; my robe a cloudy stream
The controls in my hand, a sceptor
To fly far beyond my dreams.

My kingdom has no end, my journey has no limits
In a world all my own
With time unmeasured by minutes.

I am lord of the air, pilot of the skies
Am I to be the last sound heard
By man before he dies?

*****

King of all creation, Master of men's souls
My throne the realm of Heaven
Where no silvery jet may go.

My crown, the sun; My robe, clouds of glory
Eternity I hold in My hands
As a precious dove before Me.

Paradise, My kingdom, where the souls of men ascend
To live forever more
In My peace without end.

I am Lord of the universe, Pilot of the skies
I shall be man's salvation
Just before he dies.

Micki Freels

HOW DARE THE SUN

How dare the sun shine brightly above me?
How dare the brook flow sparkling and clean?
How dare the breeze feel caressing and gentle?
How dare the fragrant grass glow emerald green?

Clouds should be shrouding the sun, bleak and somber.
Waters should hide under ice dull and gray.
Winds should be keen-edged, biting and numbing.
Grass should have long ago withered away.

All earth must mourn for the one I saw dying,
Not here beside me, but half-worlds apart.
I saw him crawl painfully, seeking a refuge,
His death cry forever burned in my heart.

But still the sun shines brightly above me,
And still the brook flows sparkling clean.
The soft breeze still feels caressing and gentle.
Still fragrant, the grass flows emerald green.

Carol A. Frey

BLACKTOP DANCER

Metal collides in the chromium glide
So deep and so wide
With nothing inside
Melting each smile
Into puddle and pile

Wheels spin for a while

People wave and they smile
getting high all the while
As the man in a glide
Quickly flies by
Taking one final ride
He ends in a pile of twisted machine
The matter obscene

little boys dare to dream

Carl Fritz

HOMO SAPIENS

The lust of our illusions dies out with our days
But no sooner have we done with one
When we fall into a new, more massive maze
Of dizzying deceit, delirium and deprivation.

Fight as we may to free us from the farce of
  fabrication
We rush into another pet and pitiful delusion,
Much like a fish is rushing after bait!
No doubt: To be a fool is man's perennial fate.

Hugo Gabriel-Freeman

CENTURY FARM

I cannot possess this land
where centuries loom,
ghosts of early settlers work:

their presence greens
each blade of grass,

each rock, a face
each tree, an old man
gnarled, time-rutted.

I see their hands
at the rusted plough,
their voices ride the wind:

there is no joy beyond
existence.

They are here,
telling my uneasy tread.

This well of history
is their keep -

I have no holding here.

Betty Sanders Garner

WE SIP WINE OUT OF PORCELAIN CUPS

We sip wine out of porcelain cups,
while I work on a square of canvas;
the silver needle slipping in and out
like a fish, the purple wool its tail.
Some of my older pieces bear poems,
in colors stolen from Van Gogh.
An elephant drawn by a child on blank
canvas long ago, now a pillow, rests
on a bed, not to be leaned against or sat upon.
As dusk falls, we lay aside our stories.

Jean Garson

BREAKERS

Out where the blue Pacific
Rises in green translucent swells.
(Momentary stained-glass panes of vert)
White sea horses spring from out the deep.
Wild-eyed, spume-manes flying,
Snorting, shrill-neighing, stampeding.
Pawing the surf in a thundrous surge
To dissipate in foam upon the shallows.
Out of the green froth like a phoenix
Rises a line of chorus girls,
Young, innocent, and inexperienced,
Shaking white ruffles of their petticoats
In Cancan.
The line breaks from the verdant stage
And metamorphases into a crowd
Of laughing children, hand in hand
Scampering to the shore,
Frightening the young gulls
Digging for land crabs in the sand.

Alice Marie Gentert

PUZZLE

I can't seem to get organized.
Books overflow bookcases
But they're old friends.
Friends aren't discarded.
Mail accumulates
Despite occasional attempts to catch up
Answer letters, write checks.
One ploy helpful:
If my name or road is misspelled
I throw it out.
That cuts down the flood
But the trickle continues.
My attempts at an abundant life
Must be too comprehensive.
What to eliminate?
Not art
Or bowling
Or church
Or the farm
Or Literacy Volunteers
Or music
Or photography
Or reading
Or writing.
Just resignation to imperfection.

Katharine Ryder Gibson

LATE AFTERNOON THUNDER STORM IN SPRINGTIME

A teasing shower and tentative rumblings
disturb my afternoon nap.
I slip back into sleep,
am scared awake
by a cataclysmic crack of thunder.
Through the window I see
darkness black as the plague
upon Pharaoh and his people.

Was the sun annihilated
by that doomsday boom?
Will the world drown
in this snare-drumming rain?

The storm whirls off.
On the horizon light shyly appears,
spreads, casts shadows,
dances on the wet leaves of trees.
A rainbow,
disjunct at the apex,
arcs across the dark dome of heaven.
God dries His sorrowing tears,
gives us yet another
of a diminishing number of chances
to live in peace,
to love one another.

Edward Goldman

FOR EVERY MONKEY CHILD

For every caged-up monkey child
we must produce a bit of wild
Limb-laddered tree where he can flee
when danger signs alert escape
from massive human hurt.

A tree to monkey up and find respite
from lemming urge freeway kills
and all our over crowding ills a friendly
tree where he can astronaut alone
or with a friend spend the night
or afternoon exploring skies the stars
and mocn escape from ghetto walls
urban sprawls peeple blight
where he can claim his own birthright
vision fuzzy-free set on infinity...

We must produce a living wild
for every caged-up monkey child!

Lola Beall Graham

ELEGY

I saw the savage waves that marked the place;
I saw the wingbeats of a homing flight.
But after the tide's turn the waves
Were pulled back to the ocean's heart.
And here in the morning stillness
Sea gulls are flying whit.

Thus you turned to a signal that I missed
I only heard the waves erase the sky.
Now hushed as a child that sleeps out
Its tears, the sea is calm at last -
Too still to shake the pale
Sea-flowers where you lie.

I hear the sea bird's call faint and far
Where now the radiant sunrays are falling;
A call, as to a new-found wanderer -
Or could it be my own heart
Calling under the breath,
Calling you, and calling.

May Gray

COURAGE AND FAITH

For all the conflicts in the world
There is progress
For all the failures in a field
There is success.

And when you're about to give up
after many years
Maybe cry a little
But don't give in to tears.

For every tear you shed
The sun will shine so bright
That in the chilly winter mornings
You won't feel the bite.

So remember everything
Will work out for the best
Believe in yourself
And let God do the rest.

Daryl Jo Greenwald

FEBRUARY

The word is a death chant
the wind shouts at the windows.
It brings death without holiday,
toppling the ornamental trees,
tightening the grip of snow.
It mocks the hope of spring,
a world of leaves and birds I imagine,
and imagining, ask,
"Where is Jimbo keeping himself?"
The wind pounds his death into my ears.
It brings the tears to my eyes.
My heart beats the rising despair
of February, February, February ...

Andrew J. Grossman

A CARVED PLANK

Shortly before the break of day,
Contending with frost goblins,
I made my way upward
Steadily, through dense brush,
Mountain laurel and pines,
Until all at once I stood
On the highest mountaintop.
Looking out across cloudland,
I marveled that up here,
I was alone with God,
Or whoever the Pretender is,
And standing above the earth,
Yet anchored to it still,
I felt a kind of airy fancy,
Shut off so from reality,
Floating away on this fragment
Of a wreck of a world,
On a carved plank in a cloud ocean,
It was a country one might
See in dreams, or perhaps,
In paradise.

Dorys Crow Grover

THE HAUNTING

Stealthfully unseen, blackest realm,
emerging in whisper inner sanctum
specter springs. Netherworld demon
unleashed haunting the conscious demeanor.
Howling ghoul, jaws seizing flesh
beyond bone. Hideous face all too true
seeing past and past again.

Mind and body, burning soul, handily
gripped by relentless knarled creature's claw.
Squeezing stone dry a drop of blood
lapped up, forked tongue spits in the eye.
The beholder trembles before majestic
terror. Royal proclamation fearsome dread
inside out looking in.

Face to face brutal awakening the force
reckoned. Recognize the battered monster
consumed in evil vengence. Fires lick
flames blacker engulfed in fear.
See the haunting face mirrored.
Recognize the battered monster
within within.

Robert G. Hadad

HIGH MEADOW SENTINELS

My mother loved these
ancient bolders--said there
is something eternal
the way they hug
the high meadows of the
mountain, and stand as
sentinels rock-watching time.

For a lifetime I've
seen the way they iceberg
themselves into the earth's crust,
solid with time's passing,
losing only what the wind
sniffs away into dust.

Another generation is
now watching these boulders,
eyeing their steadfastness
as I move to the meadow's
edge, soon ready to join the
gnawed-away dust of oblivion.

Ralph Hammond

- AND THE GREATEST OF THESE IS LOVE.

We say we love, what do we really say?
A glib trite statement, made at best to those
With whom we socialize, perhaps admire
But do we really mean love, what is meant?
Good feelings, wishing well, maybe to care
How he or she is coping with a problem;
Do we really want to be involved?
To reach out, comfort give a friendly hand
To those who hunger, homeless, those in pain.

What is this love, a pale elusive thought?
It should be doing, caring, being there
When all else fails, it goes the extra mile
Wherever one is needed, it supports, affirms
An honest love reciprocates itself
And truly does, because the more one gives
The giver, too, receives in some mysterious way
The blessings he has sought to emulate

Love is indeed beyond our human concepts
It is a gift that has its roots in God.

Margery Harper

CROSSROADS

From where I stand near the top
of the great dividing line,
I can see both ways.

On this side, my grandson Jon,
in his sandbox,
is designing hopefully
a septic system for hazardous waste.

On the other slope I can trace
my grandfather, Hiram,
gently gliding in his swinging chair,
and on the luxuriant lawn beside him,
his shepherd dog, reclining.

I cannot see beyond Grandpa,
but I can hear the chatter of chickens,
the honking of geese,
the grunting of hogs,
through the uncrowded air.

Beyond grandson--
Is that parched earth? Fetid smog?
A mushroom cloud? Hurry, Jonny!

Elva Ray Harris

CREATION

At my birth
heaven above sang
with great joy
at the thought
at my potential to be
with humanity.

The Lord touched
my soul with His grace
and marked my
heart as His
so to identify
all of His children.

At my birth
my journey of life
began and
started the
human process of finding
what lies beyond death.

Miriam Hasert

LITTLE MAN

Little Man how fast you grew
And went the way all children do
Into a world you've yet to know,
You needed room to stretch and grow.
I watched with pride as you felt your way
And tested strengths in work and play.
We shared our fun as buddies do -
When you were cut I bled some too.
Shooting the rapids or climbing high
Gazing at stars in a western sky;
We gave it our best no matter the cost
And won more times than we ever lost.

I'll always treasure those memories past,
Could prayers but make the good times last.
But boys were meant to grow up strong
And Daddies can't just tag along.
So I hope you know and understand -
I'm always near if you need a hand.
And of all God's gifts could I choose but one ...
It would be a Father's love for his Son.

C. David Hay

TEMPLES

We build You temples, Lord,
Of wood, concrete and brick and stone
But all the while, we know
Those of flesh and blood and bone,
Whether yellow, white or black or brown
Or combinations showing other tone,
Are the ones You love the best
For You made them for Your own.

Thelma C. Henshaw

I AM SMASHED

I am smashed against the ground
like the last beer drunk in darkness
broken, bleeding on your conscience
and I glitter on the pavement
somewhat tragic in the sunlight
for awhile, until I'm nothing
just a missing from your "Exports"
just a girl you used to know.

Krista Heggie

NOT QUITE LIKE MINCEMEAT PIE

They sit there by the fire, snockered,
Gently snockered to the gills,
Angry, I was not there to see,
Them show off their Christmas tree.
Do they ever stop and think, what it's like,
To spend a million holidays, in the car,
On some highway, on some rain-slick highway?
On an icy thoroughfare? Going to another's house,
So they can have their family near?

Do they ever stop and think,
Do they ever really care, what it's like,
To leave your home, your fire, your feast,
Because they want their family near?
Can they think it further, then,
Can they do a follow-through?
As you return, and turn your key, no bells,
No Christmas smells will greet you, no, not you.
Alone and cold, your memories bold, for days untold,
The silence stinging in your ear.

"Dear," I hear, "just do as you please."
What pleases me would not set well,
For I would do things differently.
"I'm staying home, what the hell."
I'm doing Christmas differently,
Doing Christmas differently.

Sara Marie Hogg

FOOD CHAIN

Black as a squid's retreat,
Marsh hides its secrets
In inky water.
Heron's lunch will find no safety
In the dark.

Patience wears a long cloak
And heron a long beak.
Together they outwit
The frog.

Barbara C. Houghton

OUT OF THE CHRYSALIS

Before we ever met
I had a life of sorts,
uncomplicated making do
with what there was at hand
not craving nectar out of reach
nor promises too lovely to believe.

Yet emergence proved quite easy
when the sun-warmth of your smile
persuaded latent wings to soar
beyond an unimagined reach
exchanging dreary dormancy
for this rainbowed atmosphere.

If ever you should leave
I would manage somehow
to fold and fit bright wings
inside an outgrown shell.

Dorothy R. Howard

THE TONGUES OF YESTERDAY

Today the old world begins with yesterday
As winter snows melt into spring,
And summer fun vanishes into the tides
Rolling out upon a bigger sea of reflection.
Instances have no fame nor memories,
Yesterday is the only recorded history.
Joys we once had
Are smothered in the space age.
The happenings of a yesteryear
Are only thoughts of, "Did it happen here?"
"Is it all a figment of the imagination?"
Or, is it a longing to be resolved
And taken back to where
Life had order, harmony, and purpose?

Nancy S. Hundley

EDEN VALLEY

Looking for love, I walked in the lovely weather
Of morning marvelous out of the winter woods;
And the young trees sang to me their greening words
Of marsh and meadow where all day long I was
One with the wind and the warmth and the wonderful.

I leaped with the small fish climbing against the current,
I tried to ride on the air, I was every creature
Of feather and fin and skin as I danced in their chorus.
Longing for love, I joined in the chirping and chanting;
I was young, I was yearning, I had no more voice than a
    cricket.

Learning to love was a torment of shaking and stirring.
I was caught like a leaf in a swirl of frightened spinning,
Like a moth sucked into a flame, or a pupa splitting;
I was naked and numb and exasperatingly stupid.
And I stumbled and fell with my fingers clutching a shadow.

But after a time or more I woke full of meaning
And went in the shining and up to the misty mountain,
Shaking my hair in the wind as I gathered mementos:
Pressed rose petals and braided branches of myrtle.
Trinkets and treasures I had and never too many.

It was late in the night when the wind died down in the valley
The dog had buried his bone and no one knew where.
The wandering over and nothing left to wonder,
Weary I stood alone in the doorway, watching
As the white moonflowers wilted, one by one.

Evelyn Tooley Hunt

THE SPIDER WEB

I saw a spider web today
resplendent in a christmas basket twined
I looked and thought should I delay
in breaking what appeared to be a
special find.

The sun it shone so crystal clear
through those dainty strands which
stretched
from handle down to the basket edge
Transfixed, I stood as I saw the beauty
etched.

The beauty of each strand was enhanced
By the light of the sun its endless rays
On each strand, a rainbow danced.
Colors so fine, they caught my eye
in so many ways.

The only way to break that-glorious
sight
Would be to wait until the sun did
ebb
and set behind the lake & trees at
night
leaving another memory of God's
glory in the spider web.

Lawrence Hutchinson

MADONNA

A newborn babe is held to her breast,
Still cuddled long after he ceases to suck.
Her thick soft hair flows over her shoulder,
Echoed by the down on his head.

So gently she rocks, soothing her son
And herself with each movement,
That they seem to be one again,
Still joined in body and in breath.

The light has gone, but yet she rocks on,
Fearful to waken or move him.
This is her purpose, her life's goal:
The madonna of the rocking chair.

Linda Hutton

SETTING LIMITS

A chauvinist cat, like a proprietor,
has intruded into my life and taken over.
He acts familiarly, tumbling my books,
and, strangely, looks like my departed lover.
He behaves as that one dead, returned from the grave,
might stalk rivals under the bed, in nooks.
Satisfied, he deems to bless the room,
letting me know the master has come home.
Tail up, imperious, he heads straight for,
and confiscates the most comfortable chair.
He falls asleep, purring, remembering.

Awake, he finds his old slippers and pokes in a paw.
He claims the sunniest spot, where my violets sit,
knocking over their pot to warm his back.
Just in time I rescue my delicate China.
I work quietly not to disturb his rest,
whole he is purring, dreaming, remembering.

When I take the ancient ashtray down,
long unused, once piled to heaven with butts
his eyes gleam. He studies me quizzically,
and then disdainfully, as lover did
whenever I said, "No smoking in this house!"
In this, at last, I shall remain supreme.
No need for grumbling, I only pour in cream.

Hyacinthe Hill

UPON LEAVING THE FARM

How this room has broadened
since then
When, with a lump in my throat
I packed my youth
not too neatly
into little deep boxes
and prayed for its keep.

How this room has dimmed
since then
before I looked upon dark betrayal
at the bookshelves
now empty
reminding me of how I never could
find a pen ...
when.

Bruce K. Johnston

OLYMIPICS

Olympics, --
Winter, --
Skiing, downhill, jumping, --
Skating (You know they can't do that
On ice
And still stay right side up),
Luge (they used to call it sled),
Curling,
Hockey, --
Still, the greatest thrill
Is when you see the maple leaf,
And hear the band
Playing familiar music
That brings you to your feet.

James Asa Johnson

SPRING OFFENSIVE

Suddenly he was there
Filling up the swamp
With raucous whistling --
His biological clock
As punctual as the
Vernal Equinox.

Where he wintered
I know not,
But now his haughty eyes
Glare with the determination
Of a General Patton.

Flashing orange epaulets
He flits among the canebrakes
Labeling his territorial boundaries.

Madolyn Jamieson

COCOON

Encased in chrysalis of snow,
Suspended in quiet timelessness
I am contained this winter day,
Content to be alone.

Permit me sit enclosed by glass,
White phantom forests on each side;
Permit me stir my gentle fire
And dream dreams in its warmth.

Do not disrupt my solitude -
This cherished respite given me -
A little while I would have peace,
Wrapped in my quiet cocoon.

Sally Jordan

ARMAGEDDON.

Destructive science moves too fast,
How can our civilization last?

The sword of Damocles hangs overhead,
All of us live in constant dread.

Is our destruction already arranged?
Or will it come as the whim of a mind deranged?

If Beings land from outer space
They'll find no trace of the human race;

Only decay and dismal dust,
Melted rubble, chaos and rust.

Poisonous gas will fill the air,
All will be gone and who's to care?

The nuclear battle is over and done ---
Who's left to say which side had won?

Alice Whiteside Jorg

THE FARM

Mid Mountain farm: gaunt, cavernous tonight
A dried-out husk of expectations, of country joys
And gladsome kitchens-now packed away with the Rodales
In the cleared-out living room. It's time to go.

Irrelevant, a stranger, I move
In the unaccustomed void
A shriveled peanut rattling about
In an oversized shell
While the toilet irritatingly drips
And the phone sits ebony still-
A vivid mute.

Outside-another world
Vibrant, moistly alive, electric with growing things
The sprinklers chug-chugging the final harvest
Pale rows of weaving ghosts
Caught by the moonlight.

Out there- owl hoot. Alarming. Quick.
A sudden rustle in the corn...
The warm earth heaves a damp sigh into the night
That mingles with the stars.

I almost envy the field mice
Ears pricked alert in the watchful dark
Doing their mousey gathering
Unconcerned with absences
Or the stoney silence of phones.

Stuart Judd

THE OLD BROWN WOMAN OR 'MY MOTHER'

The old brown woman
With a hoe in her hand
Bronzed by the sun
Part of the land
Never seeing
Never Caring
For the world
Rushing by
Clouds of dust
Billowing up
Turning everything white
Except the Old Brown Woman
With a hoe in her hand ----

Fay Kaestner

"TO GIVE MAN BACK TO HIMSELF"

A life of ease, charmed by muted voices,
Eliot was a poet of philosophy.
Real life, the life of poetry and love
Lies secret at the center of our existence,
Impervious to analysis.
He wanted to give man back to himself,
Willing to accept the facts
About the human race without despairing.
In "The Waste Land", the central character
Covert and masked, is the very poet, Eliot,
The human soul, lost in earthly limbo.
But poetry means perserverance
And the promise of resurrection.
Seeking the beautiful, the good, the true,
In a sterile and stifling urban life,
He remains passive and uncommitted.
Alone with himself and his futility
And the scars of disappointment;
The terrible awareness of his isolation
From every other human being.
Speaking many allusions,
Borrowed droppings from the dead past.
Drowned by dull inaction
He but advances the ancients' fears.

Ray Keller

SONNET XXIV

Ah Christ, you died & took your world to hell,
down to the shades & darkness where those souls,
who lived & died before the archangel fell,
who burn in ice & brimstone & white coals.
Did your sweet presence quench the devouring flame?
Was an end put to their eternity?
Could they express their joy because you came?
Or had that torment leached humanity?
So great a cloud of witnesses arose
that heaven's gate opened & all angels sang,
the spheres proclaimed His glory; the dread woes
were vanquished. The new souls as lighting sprang
through the dark spaces to eternal lights
they were most welcome in the Father's sight.

Anna Kirby

LINES FROM A POINT OF NO RETURN

Your departure day was liquid
unchanneled currents
and whirlpools
overfull nimbi
    river
    eyes.

Intervening days desiccated
tasting of dust.
Wild hemp
secreted the bitter angle
of upended skiff
of loneliness.

Today
rampant river returns
wooing the boat
as I wade to meet you.

Thelma Scott Kiser

THE ASSIGNMENT

After the phone call, the glass and the gas,
the ambulances and the bystanders, only a plastic green garbage bag.
In it someone had tossed the shoes.

They'd been driving home for Easter, watching for white dogwoods,
two teens in a back seat, their Mom and Dad up front.

Around a curve a drunken woman giggled, jiggled when he tickled;
she fought him off and dared him. In court they called it playing
chicken in a car that split my brother's car in two.

My father called. Four planes later I came home. Neighbors
brought the garbage bag, a broken suitcase of blood-dyed clothes.

"Wash the clothes," my father assigned.
"They'll need their Easter best. And match their shoes."

I took the plastic bag and trembled at white high heels, brown high
heels, tan rubber soles, size thirteen oxfords, half a lace.

Once I'd given an assignment: choose shoes for Shakespeare's characters.
"Juliet - in slippers, clogs, or spikes?" I asked.
"Romeo?" "Adidas," students said. "Lear on the heath?" "Boots by LL bean."
"Rosencrantz and Guildenstern?" "Wingtips black and blue."

Now from a garbage bag I had to choose. We carried six matched shoes
to the funeral home. We buried them that Easter Monday afternoon.

The two shoes left I polished, held them close, tried to issue
tenderness, reconfirm the instincts, meanings in the choice.

But then I learned my inability to clothe a soul. "No," said the daughter
white on her bed. "These are my mother's. Where are mine?"
"She's wearing yours," I said. "She's warm beneath the snow."

Mary Sue Koeppel

GERANIUMS IN WINTER

reach for sun,
sprout small blooms
in memory of summer,
thirst for rain,
a spider's transitory
touch, feel of turning
worm, concern of birdsong,
sound of droning bee.

Expected to perform
in winter's drying heat
they turn away dispirited,
out of season,
obsolete.

A cactus
on the other hand
makes few demands,
remains impervious
to long neglect,
thrives in sand.

And yet -
geraniums in winter
promise green pastures,
turning earth, Spring,
hope, benevolent sun,
every newborn thing.

Lynn Kozma

ANSWER TO T.S. ELIOT

To him who says this world will die
With a whimper,
I say never.
This world is filled with heroes
Without medals,
With saints whose haloes are not seen
By the naked eye,
And men who send their monuments
Beyond the stars.

Elsie Bowman Kurz

BLOODROOTS

The bloodroot blooms were gone! How bare
The woodlot looked! I searched but found no white
Star-petaled heads to peer at me. And where
They were last spring were but dry leaves. Their plight
I pondered on and wondered, were they pulled
Last year by little hands who did not know
They could not bloom again? We are unschooled
To Nature's way of things that live and grow
In woods, and take for granted, far too much,
The warbler's song, the rushing of a stream,
Blue skies, clear lakes and sand that's warm to touch.
Will these be found someday only in dream?
But then, "Bloodroots are up," my young son cried!
If so, there still is hope! I rushed outside...

Inge Logenburg Kyler

IMPART TRUTH

Be quiet,
Be still,
And let the Lord
Your soul to fill.

Think deep,
Think long,
Then let your pen
With point so strong.

Speak loud,
Speak clear,
Impart the truth
For all to hear!

Bette F. Lafferty

SUPPOSE A ROSE

Suppose a rose was all there was
to seek for, day to day.
Imagine that was all it took
to take your cares away.

What if that was all you needed
To give a stranger cheer,
Or heal a family torn apart
And finally bring them near?

Somehow I see the rolling land
Awash with crimson stands,
Neighbors reaching out to help,
Nations touching hands.

Now we all know mere flowers can't
Perform such acts as those.
But if you see a frown on a friendly face,
Reach out...and replace it with a rose.

R. J. Larson

FOURTH DIMENSION

This is the moment I would capture:

This finite point in time
along the infinite, eternal line from then till now,
colored
by its intersection with its place,
in space. Here
is the moment, Now
the place,

When where I am
is how the light strikes water,
how the wavelets splash the deck;
how,
when the sails snap,
curving the blue perimeter of sky
and bending the sheets toward water,
cool wind spills against my face -

This is the every place,
Now, the eternal time.

William P. Latham

JAZZMAN

You are elsewhere; the knowledge
of property is a must for all loans made.
Promises fulfilled: the room conducts
itself differently; the wine bottle lies
empty and bed covers rest in a tangle
of meetings and parting so like night
attempting to escape day. I cite
to your ghost not listening the meaning
of the scheme, of the contract signed
with kisses and consent and everything
except the clock holds its breath.
The phone rings isolated like a tenor
soloist. I answer like a jazzman
with improvisations; your voice sounds
distant and cluttered with thoughts
of others, but each tone tells
my ear that the song is not finished.

L. Bradley Law

BENEATH THE FISHERY WHARF

A tugboat grunts, churning up muck.
Beneath the fishery wharf
Where I'm camped, no one sees
The cigarette coal light my face.

This blanket of darkness suits me.
Shredded newsprint lines
My nest snug as any room
For rent downtown. Tubeworms

Make better neighbors anyhow,
They're quiet at night
And never pry. Mussels thrive here.
Railway spikes fetch twenty cents.

And don't the starlings catch fire
At dawn, flocking to scour
Boxcars for grain. As smoke
Carries ash from foundry stacks,

The bay winds billow birds
Out the wharf-piles.
I whistle softly and watch.
All the world is scudding, gathering.

Paul J. Lindholdt

FAMILY PROTRAIT

They lived in great grandfather's house
Four brothers and their sister
Uncle Quince, Albert, Morris, Sherman and Aunt Alice.
The brothers worked the farm, planted crops
Chopped wood, cared for the stock.
Aunt Alice cooked the meals, washed clothes, mended socks.

They never laughed
They never cried
They never lived
They simply died
One by one

The hearse carried them away
To be buried in the family plot
Overlooking their farm
That strangers own today.

Ramona G. Lipka

ANGEL OF MERCY

The hours are long both day and night
She's on her feet from ward to station
Checking temperatures, pulsations, and giving medications

Times are dreary and often sad
With LPN and orderly absentions
But caring for the ill makes her glad
To have chosen this great profession

She's always on hand when the doctors call
To give help wherever needed
But when supplies are essential for her work
Her requests are often unheeded

When a covered cart is drawn down the hall
Which is known to carry a body
Down the rear elevator it always must go
To avoid going through the lobby

For better or worse, this dedicated nurse
is from a breed that is a rarity
And that is why, she is known worldwide
To be an Angel of Mercy

Richard C. Losh

BY DAY SHE SITS POISED

By day she sits poised
behind the typewriter
Her clothes immaculate
Her posture correct
Her manner efficient.
She is such an integral part of the office
that many times her employer
forgets she does not belong to him,
like the typewriter, the desk, the file cabinet.
"My girl will get it" he says over the telephone
"the girl" who is now in her 40's
hair edging grey
efficiently conducts the office business.
Is there any other life?

Celia S. Lustgarten

GOD'S PEACE

Sparkling waters
Glisten in the sun
As waves roll
And rise higher with the winds
While breakers pounce upon the rocks
Spewing sea foam
Past where high tide mark begins.

Tempestous sea,
Did anger or despair
So rile you
That you poured out your might
To break the boundaries set by God --
"This far you go,
Beyond is not your right."

Like us,
Sometimes the sea rebels
But afterwards peace takes place.
This peace -- ours too
If we would not pull against the hands
That bless us with His grace.

Lois MacGregor

THE SOMME

a river in france
at first light
on saturday morning
july 1, 1916
the:
old boys of eaton and harrow
old boys of the king's school
sheffield pals
west yorkshire regiment
christ church boy's high school cricket team of 1908
15th highland light infantry from glasgow
church lads of the royal rifle corps
wiltshire regiment
and many, many others
stood up
went over the top
across the chalk plains
through the wheat fields
and the woods
towards the german wire
and eternity

William Macrae

POETRY'S THREE 1965

First Frost, now Eliot, then Pound;
Three who made their world of words renowned;
And spanned, from graceful simpler years,
Our age, until this present time of tears.

They roamed the range of thought and theme;
Their figured speech and innovation seem
Held within a gripping sea of doubt
With not a single port of hope about.

Excepting of an ancient, slender Light
That beckons still across the empty night,
And grants suggestion in its timorous ray--
The lone perhaps of some fair future day.

'Tis Eliot who says he sees it clearly;
Out there upon the Rock and nearly
Covered by the wash; a peek of morn
Beyond the thresh of storm and scorn.

But Frost with whimsy and his kind of care
Refuses to see what he's not sure is there;
Yet will not say it could not be
But only that it's something he can't see.

Poor Pound disdains the whole affair
And whips his arms and bellows at the air;
His is no rhyme or reason from the start,
But brilliance boasting in an unsure heart.

John Manier

FINALE OF LOVE

Remembering the purity of fledgling love
gingerly spreading untried wings
while held so tenderly in its grip
like heady wine, bubbling uninhibitedly
fragile, untried, mystifying

A pristine love, suddenly grown taut
under the awesome strain
of profound desires, unrequited
taking a savage hold on barren souls
through anguished months

A flawless love, seemingly staunch
infinitely revealing, unremorseful
tortured minds no longer in agreement
silent lips, once enticingly tender
now screaming banalities, in spurts

A tainted love, fermenting unrelentlessly
festering unbidden in aching hearts
pulling loose with unguarded finality
torn asunder by misguided trust
steeped, in overwhelming deception, bitter....

Rosebud Manis

PIER PLAYMATES

Oh mighty wave upon the ocean
When you've splashed against the pier
And pressed your bosom to the sand
Where do you go from here?

Do you roll around forever
Pushing boats up to the docks
Or do you take time out to play
And dance among the rocks

Are there times when you are angry
And you raise your arms to fight
To slash against the ships broadside
And push its bow from sight

When you've rescued baby fishes
From the fisher's savage spear
Please, tell me mighty ocean wave
Where do you go from here?

Fern Marsh

LOST

It's not in my purse, or my coat pocket, or in my top drawer.
I've lost it, yet I don't know what-
What am I looking for?

I look under the bed, beneath the chair, and behind the door.
I've lost it, yet I don't know what-
What am I looking for?

It's not on the piano, or on the table, or on the storage room floor.
I've lost it, yet I don't know what-
What am I looking for?

Frustrated and impatient, I scan through the bookcase.
My eyes are getting sore. There--covered with dust--is my Bible!
I've found my faith in the Lord.

Sulynda Martin

THIS THAT ENDURES

Steam into water, cool the flame,
Freeze the water and ice remains;
The ice as it melts evaporates
And falls to earth in the form of rain.

Tree from acorn, flower from seed
Breathe air, draw light on which to feed;
Stem of the flower, trunk of the tree,
Roots in the ground again earth will be.

Dream into man, body from tree,
Water and air for him to breathe;
Senses in man so man can see
His flesh is of earth but dream remains free.

Vivian L. Martinetz

MOTION

Clouds are just a vapor
Floating in the sky;
Clouds are like a whisper,
Clouds are like a sigh.
They blow across the graying mist,
On a blustery, windy day;
And often look fierce and awesome
When a storm is on its way.

I look up to the heavens,
And see them moving there;
Clouds against an azure sky
Seem almost like a prayer.
Float on, pretty cloud-puffs,
All across the sky;
Oh that I were winged,
I'd go with you on high.

Mary Elizabeth Matthews

THIS, A COLOR THAT NEVER WAS

Carnelian blushed
Cranberry bruised
Lustrous opalescent pearled hue

Rain-weighted green
Only in an aqua-spun dream
This, a color that never was

Dandelion yellow
Queen Anne Rose-red
Whispers of violet jasmine rush over my head.

Plum purple buried deep in my heart
Piercing silver touched steel-blue sharp,
splintering brown enriched wood like a
penetrating dart.

This, a color that never was.

Deep ebony, scintillating bronze,
Orange,
baked, overdone by Florida sun.
Antiqued not, nut ever new
Reborn of a master's formula
This, a color that never was.

Maria Jan Matula

ETHEREALITIES (2)

In dreams within dreams
I saw suns
starring as moons
on the stages of heaven
stumble and descend
through abysmal spirals.
Infinite numbers
of understudies
moved up one place,
In dreams within dreams
it was so.

Ruth O. Long Maunders

THOUGHTS OF A PEW SITTER IN ST. JOHN'S

On my birthday-
I attended a funeral
Of one like me-no more
No less-but one whose years
Had come to an end.
How did he use them?
How have I used mine?
I saw his end as my own-
His death has diminished me
And has taken away a part of me.
As I was - and am so much as he-
He was-and now is not-to our
Discerning eye-yet he is-
To those that have gone before him-
And shall receive me.
I and he are no different-but
He has completed his earthly
Journey-and mine is still
Underway-for how long-
I know not-Earth is still
Fair and close to me-Heaven
Is his and he a part of it.
One day I shall be as he-
And make the transition-which
Shall not be as apparent to
Me -as to those that are
Left behind-wondering
Where I have gone.....

Walter Mayberry

600 PICKENS STREET

At the foot of the hill
Where we used to play
Is a chapel for students
To gather and pray.
As they bend on their knees
To repent of their wrongs,
When they stand up to praise
And to sing holy songs,
I wonder if memories
Of children at play
Are blended with thoughts
Of students who pray.

Katherine Cathcart McCaskill

PREJUDICE

Something empty fell into my
cracked eye full of friends
As friends may be I see them,
they see what might be me
Something lonely fell out of my
gaze on to a friend (might be)
truly to new friend.
I tried to be - all as things of
friends are seeming nice to be
(omit me)
The new friend did
left a hollow in my song where
by the garden sad crickets
cease to be, still,
With my old friends I sometimes
see that one - friend I had
hoped would be --
Oh, friend who really didn't want
any part of me I think
I might have been the best friend
of any you will ever see.
Somehow my eye is circled
whenever I think of the friend
who didn't want me.

Kathryn Stewart McDonald

SALUTE TO FATHERS

the cave man father stalked the hunting ground
keen of eye with steady hand - quietly he stood
to make his choice - then carried home the prize
to wife and child and there they shared that sacrifice
for with his strength and time and life
he had gone into the wild to do this thing

they welcomed him with open arms
a place to rest - a meal;
and dreamed together then
to make that darkened cave
into a home

what if tools of stone are gone
and supermarket aisles replace the range?
coin of realm, time clocks and banks
take mind and eye and skill
to track the bargain down and bring it back
to share with those at home

so, welcome him with open arms
a place to rest - a meal;
and build the dreams you share
or that home becomes
a darkened cave again

Sophia E. McElheny

NAM MAN

A village of blackened ash limbs
leans silhouettes against new snow,
stripes shadows across the road.
You keep your eyes straight ahead
tap the instrument panel, bank your turn.
Skin is stretched across your forehead, whitish
your breath is opaque.
A muscle in your cheek ticks
time with a land mine
buried mud-deep belly up
in a river somewhere.
Your hands claw the wheel.
My voice is child thin
here's where we used to pick strawberries
there's the old creamery!
I fold up in the barrel of your silence.
I light a cigarette and wait
for the smoke to clear.
You say, It's okay really
the road is just slippery.

Linda Back McKay

MAGIC

Once as a child
I had magic,-
Not elves or wishes
Or such-

I had the magic
Of seeing a perfect raindrop,-
Of tasting the melting sun,
And the magic of hearing
A blade of grass growing
In the spring time.

The magic was brief
And today I wonder where
It went -
That gift of seeing.

Keith McUmber

GARDEN MONKS

Monks chant, mollify words
In monotonous melodies.
Their rough robes cover from
Bald pates to toes
That move single-file
Circling the garden rows.
Air is displaced, filled
With voice that calls up green.
Break through rock.
Vibrate new life.
Sacred questions, answers animate,
Compelled to respond
To original purposes,
Rising to find echoes, shadows, sprouts.
Earth's blood the water,
Its veins rivers, streams,
Banks hold, deepen, contain, give way,
Dry up, replenish water evaporates
Falls back again.
Monks call rain,
Sing the sun,
Fill seed to expand, burst, grow forth,
Call that I,
The one who cannot die.

Elinor Meiskey

HORIZONS

Horizons! Give us opportunities today
and growth tomorrow.

A chance to work within our own frame-
work while continuing to expand the
frame's perimeter, even if only by
small increments.

Horizons are today's accomplishments.

While beyond the scene (as behind bright,
twinkly, knowing eyes) lie thoughts
and deeds yet to be verbally vocalized.

Allowing the provocativeness of the
unsaid to become a vehicle to surge
forward.

Lorraine Melanson

NIRVANA VS. CHRISTIAN LOVE

A droplet falls into the sea
And loses its identity.
A lily blooms beside a rose;
Throughout the day each splendor shows.

Joseph G. Merrell III

THE WASTE LAND

Is it a time for celebration
To live amid today's frustration
And see the things for which we care
Reduced to wrecks beyond repair?

Was Eliot a pessimist
To see such wreckage through the mist
Of world destruction and despair
And gloomy symbols everywhere?

When all the world is cold and drear,
Should poets feel compelled to cheer?
Aren't they the ones who are aware
Of desolation everywhere?

Should we expect word-pictures bright
When we are in the gloom of night,
With nothing much to bring us hope
As through the fog we try to grope?

So poets show us where we stand
As we confront our own waste land,
As we too try to find our way
To what must be a brighter day.

With faith to help us light our path
And help us face the gloom and wrath,
We can be sure that in the end
We can begin to comprehend.

George G. Merrill

WHEN I REACH OUT

When I reach out for healing,
I want to touch hands
    Which are scarred, familiar with pain,
    pierced through with nails time and again,
    cradles of babes lifted aloft,
    strokers of things furry and soft,
    flesh wherin burns heavenly flame.

When I reach out for strength,
I want to touch hands
    Calloused from work and hanging on,
    grappling with life from dawn to dawn,
    plunged in the earth, planting a seed,
    pointing the way, taking the lead,
weapons and tools, one and the same.

When I reach out for wisdom,
I want to touch hands
    Gnarled by age and folded in prayer,
    weathered by storms, well wrung with care,
    wearied by burden, free from bond,
    groping into the vast beyond
    to touch a god and know his name.

Norman Middleton

TO G. N. K. - AUGUST, 1988

How does one say the things that matter
  minute by minute
Hour by hour, day by day
  as week by week march on.
Time knows no boundaries such as we set.
It is a forward motion that never stops.
There is little rest for such as we
  where time drifts toward Eternity.
I cannot hope to know as yet where forces lead me.
There is rhyme and reason to it all -
What happens to us is left to Fate
  and our Destiny.

Phyllis Ann Miller

BROKEN SHELL

Almost two decades had faded
into the blurred gray fog of ages---
yet still the sight of a yellow ribbon
compelled Marsha Nigra's heart
to skip a beat---

Momentarily recalling poignant memories
of unfulfilled dreams
of seventeenth summer love.
Eyes riveted on padded sides of confining cage,
she stoically, albeit unconsciously,
refused to accept the reality
of senseless war
in some far-off Asian jungle.

Words of her own high school valedictory
had never predicted that his name, that life itself---
now forever etched in a symbolic wall of marble---
becomes a lingering eternity---sometimes---
leaving behind a broken shell,
a vast black emptiness,
that even time itself
cannot always heal.

Carl B. J. Minor

SLEEP

No nightmares, you said, no demons.
You groan,
a foot strikes my calf.
Your dreams are not as smooth as you dream.

Up here the air is tight, cricket-charged.
Heat rises from our hands.
We separate,
scrape down through different holes.
You name the stones down there.
At dawn you have forgotten all the names,
and the way down,
and that there is a way.

Penelope Moffet

ANGELFISH

Solitary in the sea,
This single cold heart,
Moving among the chorals
    of the tide
In transparent glory,
Shows us the beauty
Of a higher power's art.

What magic has this God
That can fashion stars
Unborn in outer space,
And mysteriously raise
And drop the tides..
What love displayed
In this creature veined,
Adorned in opal lace!

Marcia Chvat Minot

COUNTRY CATS AT HIGH HOPES

T.S. Eliot sings of City Cats,
But we, living on a farm, away from hustle and bustle,
Toast our Country Cats.

The first is Dolly-
Mostly orange with many colored rings on her tail,
Lovable and talkative - Follows me on my walks.

Next comes Monkey, a true gray tabby,
Lean, secretive and independent.
Follows me at a distance, or hides in the brush.

Then comes Trouble,
Dark grey with light grey geometrics,
It's hard to tell what Trouble thinks as he is a loner.

Let's not forget Daniel Boone - so named as he was found in
the woods,
A green-eyed ball of black fuzz,
Who, tho still a kitten, attacks everything in sight.

All are good mousers and molers, too,
But do not harm the chickens,
And keep intruders at bay.

Natalie Dagmar Montague

SUBURBAN YARDS

My parents gave each other plants
for birthdays, anniversaries
until our yard resembled
all others;
rough fences, spiny juniper tams.

The houses
inexpensive forms
of angular '50's line
white brick, turquoise walls.
Things built in,
polished pine Shaker plain
but prideful.

Paul McCobb,
my mother said. A classic.
A table, said my father
with his feet.

Behind our house, down
a shifting, sandy slope
Eastside Gravel
long abandoned and left to children.

Gathering at
corrugated slides of
torn and rusted truck beds
to eat what we could find,
crabapples, berries, sauerkraut weed,
even alder marrow.

Tying each other to soggy-rafted plywood
to pole across rainwater ponds
in stiff white jeans
bleached beyond relief.

Margit Moore

FRIENDSHIP

Have you ever given a hand to a man
and learned to call him friend
only to find as friendship ran
your hand was but means to an end?

Or have you ever given a hand to a friend
who sorely needed it lent?
Then unhappily noticed, upon using your own
that the flesh was bare to the bone.

Or have you ever given a hand to a friend
who thanked you with tears in his eyes,
but later when his asked to lend,
needed both to dry off his eyes?

The lesson clearly seems to be
keep both hands in your pocket
but friend that's living death, you see,
and here's my hand upon it.
Please leave it in it's socket!

Craig Morton, Jr.

BLUE IRIS

blue iris
should you study
    the lines on my face
the triplet arpeggios
of a sonata
    are scored there...

    you will know which one.

in return
let your mathematician
    dance past his emotions
into the pure land
of your being
        once...

and i will write you poems.

Paul T. Motoyoshi

APRIL IN PARIS

Spring in Paris, age 22, dark bars,
sidewalk cafes, can-can girls,
Baudelaire recitations, studies at the
Sorbonne, writing poetry in French,
susurrus of winnowing April breezes.
Young Tom Eliot waits for his friend
in the Luxembourg Gardens
who arrives waving a lilac branch.
And so Tom would remember and mourn
those Paris days after his friend
lost his life in the Dardanelles.
Would he be haunted
by a friendship that brief,
ever burning bright
and forever re-echoing?

LaMoyne Nations

YELLOW MOON

Yellow moon
of distant coolness
black algae fingers
slithering across
your face,
like the hidden desire
in the corners
of your eyes...

Ruth Nebbia

WHEN I CONSIDER ...

When I consider how my days are spent
In philosophic quest on spongy soil
Or futile sessions mired in precedent,
In jangling strife or ministrative toil;
When I encounter greedy, grasping men
Who mask their avaricious ways in guile,
Or selfish souls whose only regimen
Consists of egocentric ploy or wile;
When I have jounced and bounced on bumpy streets,
And threaded carefully through crowded halls
Beneath an incubus of noise that beats
And throbs until I reach my study walls;
I draw a breath, relax, and think of you,
Restored thereby to face the day anew.

Raymond S. Nelson

JUST TO BE EQUAL

Just to be equal to feathers
and seed shells would take more
than man wants to share.
He rubs his hands together
for surprise, they open to hold
nothing, nothing equal to dust
dirt is made of.

Every animal of the forest,
dying in Winter, is in a grave
or carefully digested.
Every secret of man is out,
a dead body on a wharf.

What the wind loosens goes on
to a place the earth makes.
What loose hands hold
is drawn to roadsides and
gulleys, just to be equal
to the other dancers.

Ann Newell

WHISPERS IN THE WIND

music, the comforter of the soul.
    it can draw out joy and happiness
as well as soothe a sad heart.
    for me, the calming power
of this heavenly gift
    is far greater than words.
to think that, what was once
    just a haunting sound through the land,
has become the sanctity of life
    and emotion for man.
to be given the chance to hear
    the sounds of mother nature,
in the music of the seasons,
    gathered together with love,
is an honour bestowed to a very few.
    a gentle and wise guardian
has given us the gift
    to be able to produce music
for every body, mind and soul.
    music is a direct communication
that we have with our inner selves.
    through it we can experience
all the love and devotion
    our Father feels for us.

George D. Nicholls

TO GOD

My heart is held
In Your loving hands
Like a baby in
It's mother's womb
Protected from life's cares
By an ocean of serenity
Surrounded by Your loving gifts
And my heart overflows
with love
Borne from your blessings.

Wanda Lee O'Brien

SHALL I THROW HER TO THE RAG AND BONE MAN

Rags Bones Bottles and Jars,
what will you give for my wife?
She sleeps too late and she nags too far
so what will you give for my wife?
She talks and talks in a voice so low
and she knows I cannot hear.
Mr. Rags Bones Bottles and Jars,
she does not weigh so much as you think
and she always wants me to scratch her back
and she always wants a kiss.
Shall I toss her over the balcony?
She will float through the air
in her thin nightgown.
She will catch you around the neck.
She will tell you how mean and how good I am.
I will give you a wink.

Joyce Odam

RAIN CLOUDS

Dark and verboten, clouds boil up from the horizon,
Virga hand like old soldiers' beards from the edges,

Shards of afternoon brilliance cut off the fringes and streak
past the top,
The anvil stretches net-like above the nimbus,
Then, rolling and churning, darkness tumbles over the land,

The mass moves overhead with a dull boom, and lighting
stitches the base to the earth,
Quiet, persistent, like a sheet it approaches,
Then, wet and refreshing, the cool rain envelopes all.

George Offutt

BIRTHDAY

Once a year we celebrate birth
For the meager time we spend on earth
How fast time seems to go that day
The memory balks, yet there's much to say

As we laugh at the meaning the past may have
And we hope for a while to evade the grave
Is it children we live for and retirement?
While the modern world defiles the firmament

Comfort is certainly one of our aims
As most of the world is playing games
We hope for a Heaven we cannot see
We change each year not knowing how to be

We laugh at Hell, excused from sin
By the knowledge of how "good" we've been

Michael Onida

THE SNAKE

He Told me Who He Is...
    He Said, "I Create evil;
I Made the Snake and Spoke through Him,
thus fascinating Eve.

how Beautiful my Wings
    upon that fateful Tree...

because she was beguiled,
i crawl through earth and sea."

Ellis Ovesen

PERSIMMON HILL

It was a pleasant autumn day.
'Cross the pasture we made our way.
It had not rained for sev'ral weeks,
So car he drove could cross the creeks.
He drove us to Persimmon Hill,
Where fruit was ripe from autumn chill.
Our stomachs filled, our hearts were too.
Such golden moments, life has few.
While driving there we had our fun,
And also after eating done.
While driving there she sat my lap,
And sat with lovely head laid back.
With fragrance of her my nose filled,
And her responsive body thrilled.
And all the way the trip back home,
More golden moments to us born.
Persimmon trees are now cut down.
Where once they grew is now a town.
Still in my mind I get a thrill,
When I recall Persimmon Hill.

Donald Owen

MISERY'S COMPANY

A car crashed over a bridge and
  into the river
It wasn't none too nice
But some cars slip around like that
... When they're a-facing ice.

Many cars cried sympathy
As slowly they creeped through
But another car lost it, hollering,
  "I'mmm a-coming toooo!"

Helen Paquin

BEQUEST PROTEST

Ah, could some mind, with masterstroke,
but find the watchword to invoke
greed-blinded eyes of common folk
to open wide and take alarm
at what irrevocable harm
the heedless cause without a qualm,
at needless waste of Nature's wealth,
at disregard, far worse than stealth,
that robs the innocent of health.

This Gabriel, with golden horn
should hasten Earthward to forewarn
that generations yet unborn
will reap the harvest-havoc we
are sowing daily, carelessly:
unblest bequest of our debris!

Helen Wohl Patterson

LISTENING

I am listening, still, for the echo
of his voice. It's soft, rough,
melts my soul, chills my warm body.
It's comforting like a cool breeze
on a hot, humid day- a warm vent on
a cold, winter night. It's the sound
of understanding during a moment of
heartache, a silent whisper in a
roaring, cheering crowd. It's a
smile when everything fails, a hand
when I'm drowning in a pool of tears.
I am listening, still, for the echo
of his voice. It's the sound of thunder,
the silence of night. It's the glowing
of a burning candle during a moment of
romance. I am listening still, praying
to hear his voice soon.

Virginia Patrick

LET THERE BE LIGHT

The dawn has come -
The sky streaks light -
And, lo, it is the end of night.

So is the soul
When God has come
Forever with the darkness done.

Eva Pearse

THE REVELATION

As I sit on a bench by the river's lee
With birds and bees for company
In the quiet and stillness, my mind takes flight
Like a lark winging home to his nest at night.

And my heart gives a flutter, and then stands still;
Unable to contain the fill
Of inspiration revealed by God
In Christ, but only now its facade

Opened to me, so that I could see
The Father within as an entity,
Who "Doeth the works", my own subconscious mind
Who beats my heart, digests my food, and I find

Protects my body from all ills
Real or imagined, and happily spills
His blessings to cover the inner man,
And will reign, if you'll let Him, over all the clan.

Oh, I know I wrestle with Him, and try
To have my way, and it's 'do or die'.
And He won't force me to obey His will.
Yet He'll keep on wrestling with me, until

I yield to His still, small, insistent voice.
Then, like Jacob of old, I am blessed, and rejoice
That His way led to higher ground.
Now I'm climbing the ladder, heaven-bound.

Winnifred Pearson

JESUS IS THE FRIEND OF SINNERS

Jesus is the friend of sinners,
He will listen to our plea
If we're willing to come to Him
From our sins He'll set us free.

He's the friend of little children,
All the children of the land;
He will love them and protect them,
He will guide them by His hand.

He's the friend of those in sorrow,
He's the friend of those in need;
He's the friend of the sick and lonely
If we'll only let Him lead.

He will lead us in green pastures,
He'll be with us all the way;
He will cheer us and defend us
If we'll only with Him stay.

So then let us follow Jesus
And His praises daily sing;
There's no other friend like Jesus,
He's our leader and our King.

Mabel Epes Peterson

ON CONVENT GROUNDS

An old Spruce cut down.
Limbs stiff in the snow.
A wind soars across the field
in gusts, hysterical circles
neatly arranged.

Nuns walk briskly on
the path to their Convent.
Their flapping gowns
wings against the stillness
As though to keep the order

in tact, in place. A rose
in the puffs of their breath
steams up in a cloud.
Dissipates in the air with
the memory of an old tree.

Thomas A. Phelan

PAINTING IN THE SPRING

The filmy ribbons of the dawn, such lovely pastel things,
Had just begun to drape the cloudless Eastern sky
When a mockingbird swiftly winging,
Nearly burst his golden throat while singing

His glorious morning arias to the rising sun;
In each note more beauty he seemed to bring
Until his melodious notes, a jewelled rosary, were hung
Above a world where God was painting in the spring.

Peach trees hiding under saucy rose umbrellas
Stood close beside the fragrant plum's frothing snow,
While a lone redbud, a handsome fellow,
Blossomed in the emerald meadow far below.

Each sunbeam seemed to hold half forgotten dreams
Of long past years with all their wondrous springs,
When each enchanted day, thrilling with love's old theme,
Whispered softly by on shining silver wings.

Glory Posey

A QUESTION

Do not wake the dreamer from the dream.
Let him be--there in the dark next to you--
screaming whatever agony his spirit heaves.
He must act it out--the entire carnage.
It is his part to play, his role
to work it through, night after shrieking night.
And so it was--how many years--
while I questioned that the nightmare
must go on like a stage play,
scene after scene against the same dark sky.

I did not know the backdrop nor the plot
that flashed before his eyes and shook his bones.
I only feared the warning in my ears:
Do not tear the dreamer from the dream.

One day just in time I saw him turn a page.
I caught his horror, recognition in a picture
of that fatal night, thick with comrades' cries,
their pleading faces lighted by blazing shells,
their fumbling hands pulling at his boots.
His long-borne guilt was ordered then:
Never stop. Always forward. Build a beachhead.

He told it all. And all screams ceased.
That ever-lurking foe was faced in daylight
and was gone. Again I asked, why not
gently bear the dreamer from the dream?

Judith Ahrens Powell

HAPPINESS

Birds in the sky
Ask me why
I can't fly
Then I reply
"The sky's too high.
Even without wings,
My heart sings!"

Mariana Beeching Prieto

WHEN TWO HAVE LOVED

When two have loved
    a rainbow graces
    finish lines and
    starting places.
Even broken threads can fashion
    opal lightings
    such as flash on
        cosmic gold
        that make the pattern
    of rings around
    the planet Saturn.
Somewhere, rainbows meet and widen;
Somewhere, harbors let the tide in...
    when two have lived ...
    and loved.

James W. Proctor

GRAVEYARD

There is a graveyard
near the town
And I can hear its voice
it sounds of her
Like everything poor and still.
I cannot love her
though she demands it
her shadowy kinship trumpets
-my belonging
I wonder when I will share
that peace
but my blood runs a
faded ink.

Gardiner Quartermaine

HELENA AND BACK

At the foot of the Sleeping Giant,
rattlesnakes curl in the profuse light
    of morning,
they lie like the long wicks of unlit candles
awaiting the forked flame to warm
    their many kindred circles.
We climb to the tops of mountains,
lose ourselves amid the big sky
country where hills surround us
like storm waves that rise
    upon a frozen sea.
We ride
    the crest of the highest wave,
prepare for the new sun
to light our tongues,
    with the right words
    we burn our names
    across the perfect sky.

Alfred Quarto

MY QUEST

I searched for Beauty, far and wide, for deep inside, my heart,
its music played a single tone that could not harmonize alone.
In Spring I heard a robin sing; its trilling note, a joyful thing,
a stealthy cat crept slinking by,
to kill the song, and make me cry.

Then Summer brought the cooling kiss of fountains spraying into mist,
and gently tapping my refrain, until my heart rejoiced again,
but jagged lightning split the air
while blackened clouds were grumbling there.

I wandered in a field of grain, warm with sunshine's golden flame.
My Beauty's song was lost again,
for winging in the azure sky, I heard wild geese go honking by,
Autumn would die.

I looked on Winter's frozen glow, and laughed and tumbled in the snow.
I felt the icy, north winds blow.

I saw a mountain grand and high with spires reaching to the sky,
and in beside a pillar tall, violets were clinging to a wall
still growing ...

And then Truth's cello sang my song,
its throb, in harmony along, was low: sublime, and it was mine.

My soul had touched a purple bloom all bright with dew
        and when it opened to full view
        I saw God's love ...
protecting such a tiny flower with all its power ...
        and it was Beauty!

Lorna M. Quarton

IF HE COULD CHOOSE

There were so many things that he had planned
to fill the years when he at last retired.
I wonder if his mind can understand
the cruel trick the Fates* deftly conspired
that now allows Clotho to slowly spin
a muddled cloth approved by Lachesis.
I think the trio shares his toothless grin
when they survey the broad antithesis
from what he was to what he has become ---
a diapered man of almost eighty-three
who waits with helpless patience to succumb
when Atropos is told to cut him free.
If he could choose to be alive or dead,
I know he'd end this senseless length of thread.

Linda Swift Reeder

[* the Fates, in Greek and Roman mythology, the three goddesses who control human destiny and life; the first (Clotho) spins the thread of life, the second (Lachesis) determines its length, and the third (Atropos) cuts it off.]

BEYOND THE WAVE

I told my love once
We would live by the water, beyond the wave,
And build our house high on stilts,
Of boards the sea had given up,
Eat from shells, and sleep late, with gulls to cover
us at morning,
And be awakened to sounds of bells shaken from the rocks
at twelve.
It was a simple dream but so difficult.
To build at all needs be much love, and takes a genius and
guts.
My love said, "We are Gullivers," which meant to her
That we were large in capacity, with much laughter
Between us, and each out of paradise a dawn,
Seeking that endless way home again,
The morning-star that is both a river and a way.
But the old Japanese prints were made from the whole truth.
There are floods and waves higher than men's mouths,
And in the orient they prefigure man and lose him in the
elements;
There it does not matter much if they dream little or big
events,
As long as they may hold it by the throat.

Edward Jad Reilly

SOLITARY NOMAD

Below the Arctic Circle, in a land near the top of the world
A figure huddled near a fire seeking warmth from the wind
as it hurled
Down from the polar ice caps, racing across frozen sound
White snow swirling before it, obscuring the bleak barren ground

At his back was a tent made of bear skins, thrown up in a small
copse of trees
Slightly blocking the frigid wind which brings death by slow,
slow degrees.
His dog sled was pulled up near by him, his malamutes had
burrowed in snow
Seeking relief from the blizzard which dimmed Arctic sun
to faint glow.

His tribe had journeyed far southward, migrating with the
Canada geese
He had lingered somewhat longer, now facing bitter winds
without cease
Sparks rose from the fire's dying embers, plucked up by the
wind's gusting force
Wrenching them out of the campfire, surging wind showed no
sign of remorse.

The gale had come unexpected and caught him still far to the
north
Far from his homeland and refuge, further south from whence
he set forth
He knew he must keep the fire burning, until raging squalls did
subside
Or he would never make the trek south, across the Great Divide.

He prayed that the storm would soon abate, regretted his
singular life
And his travels into the wasteland that had brought him nothing
but strife
But the storm increased in intensity and would not relinquish
its grip
Before the long night was over, the nomad had made his last trip.

Raymond Le Rendu

A HAUNTING REFRAIN

I turned my ear to the wind last night
And listened for the cry of wild geese
On an autumn night, with full moon bright
I could hear a faint call start and then cease.

An early gaggle of geese winging south
Flying high on this luminous night
Sending a message along the wind
As they soar in perfect wedge flight.

They follow an ancient path in the sky
A passage unmarked among stars
Sometimes flying above purple clouds
Always south-east of Mars.

Ever winging their way to the south
Fleeing the bleak winter freeze
Riding air currents high in the sky
With each thrust, they glide on the breeze.

Each year they repeat their migration south
Flying forth in flawless formation
Following a call, uncanny instinct
Never once a slight variation.

When the call of the wild is borne on the wind
Then I walk near the woodland at night
And listen for the cry of wild geese
As their shadows pass by in moonlight.

Raymond Le Rendu

"THOU FOOL --! thou fool"

The "VISION" is not
some opaque form
we vaguely see
The vision is the Earth --
The Life -- The Moment --
You and Me.

To apprehend the incredible GIFT
the body is the
Spiritual Tool
Most waste it on a "reality"
they never really knew
while Death's angel cries:
"Thou FOOL --!
thou fool!" ---

Helen C. Rhodes

TAO

(to Vivien Fong and parents)

In the land of the middle
called China
they say
snow is rain
you can hold in your hand
and
wind is an insect
being blown against a sail
and
Tao is the way
of Nature.

Margaret O. Richardson

PROPHETS AND MARTYRS

Drifting in upon the billowing sills
Vaulted in solace, some pose their pain like symbols
Of marble hewn to the point of their comfort,
Others embrace or praise their consummated link.
The fire they breathed, impaled on spit despising
Their tongues, endured as foreshadows of the lamp
Or as oil which burned for its history:
They cross and wounds from wreaths of bleeding roses
Arouse the core of expansion, enlightment's
Excitement suffuses musings coiling veins
Which tame the famished lions of heart's jungle
Whose passion hangs on immortality
Thundering in the eye of resolution
Washing repose through the pews of His chest.

Timothy Richardson

GEORGE AND NATASHA
(inspired by T.S. Eliot)

He strolled the brick walk
that meandered around
the lawn and flower beds,
with the assurance of a
well loved country squire.

A handsome fellow, George,
Plumey tail and golden fur
shining in the sunlight,
belied his twelve years.

He greeted us with charming
dignity; and made us feel
welcome, by a gracious
purrrring.

His mother Natasha, curled
comfortably on a cushioned
chair in the kitchen, opened
a half blind eye and peered up
as we stroked her old, grey head.

A delightful, old, feline lady -
of twenty years, having an
afternoon nap; friendly, but -
a "do not disturb me" attitude.

M. Ringereide

I TRUST

My compass fingers touch
The edge of velvet,
Petals struck against the sky.

An attraction entraps stars,
Shadows, tombs squared.
The fine gold of desire
Reaches beyond stone,
A flexible yesterday,
A volatile crossroad.

Light swarms, trembling
In silence opened
In worlds of blossoms.
A morning rose vies
For my attention,
Leans toward warmth,
Scent, the sun
Without an inquest,
Just brilliance, color
And I trust,
I trust.

Ella Robinson

KINTARO - AME

candy cane
    broken on the sidewalk -
sticky tears

Charles B. Rodning

TNT

TNT needed to blast some unidentified type.
To form a proper boarder. No reservations
& cash in advance.
Otherwise it is a wasteland.
Waiting for the axe to fall:

> "If you speak I will cut off your head.
> If you don't speak I will cut off your head."

An intense resolution.
The ears of every beast untriggered by a wind
scaled with cones keyed in ancient tonical rhythms.
A dilemma. The earth upheaving their feet
stuck in the grass or clutching branches.
Unable to disconnect Zen from Zeno.
Alice drank the lemonade, stroked the lemur,
  ran with the lemmings & would've lost her head
  except for nonsense.
No such uninvited ghost to deal with monsters
banked high in timber.
Whether Madagascar, Norway or B.C.
When the landscape disappeared beneath them.
They disappeared.

Stan Rogal

GET YOUR HEAD OFF MY PILLOW

Stretch your long frame
over there
    snore into your wall
not mine.
    I reached for you
and nearly fell on the floor so
I repeat my plea.
    What a bore.
Puff purred into your ear,
hissed her surprise all night.
All night with nothing right.
Spot clickety clicked confusion.
No profusion of sleepers,
just me and you
not you and me.
North south west east,
we made our nest.
Now put our universe
    in order.
Get your head off my pillow.

Lila Borg Rohrer

SMALL DIFFERENCES

November light spreads a sheet
behind the trees, shows home
movies of my dreams. My German
relatives rise up like smoke
from burning leaves. Their talk
of altar flowers, deadlines,
the small differences our lives make
floats up to the cloudy shell I watch
for clear light to break through.

Stubborn as old bones, the whole
family is alive and chatting
until I wake and set the memory
straight--Aunt Wilma, Grandma,
dead, Uncle Al, hovering,
a few weeks to live. Aunt Clara,
Dad, blond greying to white,
shadowing into age as imperceptibly
as darkness tarnishes the winter sky
and sleep moves us all into dream.

Judith Root

FULL OF MOON

the moon is a silver belly
swelling on the shadowed hips of space
full with night-milk
rivers drink the lunar ale
and flood the sane.

tender madness bursts
from restless schemes,
knocks pebbles into dreams
that ripple to the surface,
dancing rings around the stone

hearts, suckled on the milky wine,
beat and bay, caressed in night's wet
fold, pressed close.
the touched are taken.

through the moon's pulse runs the earth's
the rupture of the ripe,
the falling of the song,
to stain moon's milk to pink,
eclipse the belly's dance.

torment sinks, sidles into seams of sleep
the silver belly lands
splashing of the nectar dries
cooling hearts left stranded
and dreams that drown in tidal dawns
search for darker sides

Rhea Rose

ALCHEMY AT SUZHOU

We stroll through the Transforming Garden, discover rocks
the height of men; their rough heads own
see-through holes like eyes
looking opposite ways.

Our Chinese guide asks if we can name
four places where the moon may appear reflected.
In a calm lake, a mirror - I call out
"Within a man's eyes!"

Don't my own journeys mimic those
of our satellite? Full moon loves, eclipses,
crescent recoveries. Galaxies may parade
my half-guessed secrets.

Sky-reflecting, wandering alone, I meet
another rock weathering toward human form,
its head already pierced by double views;
the scarred surface reminds me

how battered the moon's face, desolate
with deserts, empty sea-beds;
the moon is a dead globe.

Dead? When I drink in its radiant promenades
the moon is born again, its silver mask
a presence moving beyond illusion
into its own beauty's body.

Rose Rosberg

WHO'D WANT TO OWN AN ISLAND?

Tom scoffed, "Who'd want to own an island? Mark
How thick the moss hangs from the cedars there;
Fof washes everything and isolation comes with dark."
"Well", Jason said, "all people love retreat
Into some kind of womb: a man might rule
that even a few days on the sun-baked rocks,
Or swimming nude in sun-warmed, sea-carved pool
Beyond the view of any human sight
Is worth discomfort of a musty bed,
Cold clammy sheets, the always rationed light."
The Cynic said," Now can't you almost hear
In drawing rooms next winter a refrain
As tiresome as a rooster's constant crowing,
"We own an island off the coast of Maine!"

Elizabeth Massie Rourke

IN MEMORY OF T.S. ELIOT

In memory of your birth
Of your time on this earth.
We remember what you have written,
And all that you have done.

Time marches by fast.
And waits for no one.
We must do what we can
In the time we do have.

T.S. Eliot you have done your share.
In the time you were here.
We remember "The Wasteland"
And your "Murder in the Cathedral."

Now we treasure your memory
Of the past gone by.
You will not be forgotten
Now in the hearts of everyone.

Ruby Rowland

VANCOUVER

Massively insensitive, the City,
Designed for cars, draws Love like blood, draws Pity.
Clad smart as print, and trendy, thoughts derailed
By the rush-hour, souls are racked and nailed
Downtown, drawn tight upon the humming wires,
Throbbing, electric, tense, and loud as lyres
Played by guitarists needing alms and tea,
But not designed for Music Therapy:
A City made for cars, not glorious bells.
All souls are private Heavens, private Hells -
Hells more than Heavens, morose more than Despair -
Rushing to work and back like soughing air;
Free, but at gunpoint; jealous of privacy -
Hugging their great, sad secrets like the Sea.
While Nature, "heartless, witless Nature," old
As the Pyramids, is grand, primordial, bold,
And smiles in brainless beauty over all.
The rooks and ravens caw: they seem to call.
Withdrawn upon Grouse Mountain, you will find
How lost you are; and love-sick, tear-blind -
Far from the dreadful din, the nuclear tone -
How terrified, how unconsoled, and how alone!

Joe M. Ruggier

THE FLOWER SEED

May these words be music to thine ears
May thy Spirit shine despite the tears
The tears that never cease to fall
From the eyes of one and all
Who dwell upon this whirling sphere
Where breaths are short and death is near
Where time is spent without regard
By men and women working hard
To do the things that must be done
Up until their course is run
Where pain and all its suffering
Outweighs the pleasures life may bring
Where man with nature wages war
By giving less and taking more
More than what he'll really need
To fertilize the Flower Seed
That has been planted in the earth
In hopes that love will giveth birth
To children of a noble race
Who won't deride their Father's grace.

Tony Santa Maria

SONG FOR ME

I walked barefoot atop the pines,
Passing you tireless in the dark
Night.
Everything has changed.
I can't remember who you are
Or what you meant to me.
There's no time for strangers,
Anymore.
Everything's in place.
As I slow the stride of my burning feet
And resist your fading voice,
Purple and blue flowers form a halo
Around a single black rose
And white birds are playing
A heavenly song.

Robert J. Savino

MIDWINTER THAW

It is the anniversary of hope, though
every seven years we should be entirely
new, every cell replaced, every dream
fulfilled or forgotten. I did not
look for flowers as I stood hunched
in a cold wind untying holiday lights
from a small tree. The only flowers
are those I give you ritualistically
before every recital, that you have
learned to wear with aplomb and indifference.
The notes are only Bach and Reger, not
private words in small envelopes. I
have made and remade my life, written
you into and out of it, carved your name
in a forest of trees and seen the
lightning erase them. Yet the music
flows on ineluctably as a major waterway
navigable at all seasons though more
approachable at some. Nearly frozen,
it takes each curve deeply and unhalting;
only permanent drought will ever stop
the flow that converts wind and ice
to power, follows the rooting of trees,
makes a mockery of all calendars.

Amy Jo Schoonover

KIEV CHILD IN A MUD PUDDLE
(1985)

Tiny boy splashing
in brackish water,
your face has remained with me.
The awe and wonder
in your innocent countenance
beneath a burning Ukrainian sun,
the day stands still.
Glowing pride in your
Grandmother's face, as she
stands watching over you,
your friendly wave
to tourists passing
through the world
of your apartment complex back yard.
Now contamination hangs
below that brilliant noon day sky.
Not as sad, your wrinkled Grandma's
coming demise. Her time
has run its course...but you!
Each morning, I arise from bed
carrying the weight
of your diminished years
between my shoulder blades.

Ruth Wildes Schuler

CLOTHES-LINE RAPE

March flings a tantrum
of cross-current wind.
Gorges on kites,
overcoats,
old paper and trash cans.

Pouts small
soughing sounds through shriveled roots
on up-turned trees.

Balloons
In sudden lust
into a virgin's sheet

looses breath,
leaves.

Clara Peck Schultz

FAMILY DOG

There are all these things
you get from a dog:
tail waggings, face lickings
continual companionship.

Now, thinking back,
I'm wondering
if we shouldn't have invited her
to our christenings,
picnics and weddings.

Deloris Selinsky

SAMSON'S FAREWELL

(Judges 16, 4-30)

No: you were not my first love, not the first
Of my betrayers, both of the accursed
Nation of Dagon worshippers. I stand,
His temple pillars here at either hand.

O my beloved, for what did you betray
Your husband on that unforgotten day?
Thrice did I lie to you, but then the truth
I told to you; could you not feel some truth?

So here am I, now blinded and in chains,
The sport of Philistines who mock my pains.
The Lord, I know, my urgent prayer will heed,
And grant me strength in my last hour of need.

O my Delilah, when all these are slain,
And Jahweh's vengeance on his foes made plain,
May he in mercy not my wife condemn -
May you, beloved, be found not one of them.

John Sewell

CASE NO. 4768

A shoe hurled...laced with slanderous reproach!
A window broken by a primal self.
Emotions spilling scarlet rivers
over walls of crumbling translucency - in ruins.

The memory still sharp, still breathing in the opponent's hand,
serving as testimony to an act
directed by tribal voices heard within,
(those apolitical ones, disdainful of enculturation).

The judge, in robes of cauldron black,
avoids his eyes, and
pronounces the defending law reprieve:
until the witches' chant is done.

He climbs steep steps toward halls of humility,
appearing so to some and so to others -
riding, reeling on gilded wings
of our law's obsequiousness.

Will payment with his soul's currency
in some dingy dusty doleful office
of appointed servants to the mind, be returned to him
in brilliance, in diamond facets, in saved face?

His accuser's eyes fill with tears,
washing clean the treacheries.

Lynda Smith

TO UTMOST BOUNDS

To utmost bounds of everlasting hills,
My soul makes plans to go, though parting rends:
Experiencing a journeying is thrills.

So I will say goodbye to homes' sweet sills
From which I've gazed beyond both friend and kins -
To utmost bounds of everlasting hills.

I leave unfinished tasks that taxed my skills,
Those unflowered plants! Some garments still need mends:
Experiencing a journeying is thrills.

Those books laid by to read many shelf-rack fills.
Pen, paper, typing waits: thoughts, might-have-beens:
To utmost bounds of everlasting hills.

A garnering of foods, boxed, prescribed pills,
All laid aside; confessed, forgiven sins:
Experiencing a journeying is thrills.

Inexorably, time fine-grinds old mills -
At last I'm lifted free of daily dins:
To utmost bounds of everlasting hills -
Experiencing a journeying is thrills.

M. Aldridge Smith

STADIUM OF YOUTH

An outsider I am ... to the Stadium.
I hear the tumult ...
I sense the carefree ecstasy ...
I taste the vividness ...
I ... I realize the false gods
the cruelty
the blindness ...

I was there.

I envy the players. No, I don't. Yes, at times.
Those who evicted me didn't know.
But I am naive no longer.
It was initiation. For out here.
The games go on without me.

Reality must be.

New rules. New old faces.
Wise I am without the tinted glasses.
Or cynical. Or just older ...
And

"I wouldn't be a kid again," said my wife.

Thomas S. Smith

ADDRESSES

A job-stray, I moved from postbox
to boarding-house, then rented rooms.
My mind did not calculate
locations, proper or not,
but floated, a bottle
on the waves of experience.

Between college terms, my grandson
travels to Mexico, to report
on the homeless, today's big issue.
"His penchant for the down-and-out
upsets us," his mother's mother
airmails with a British postmark.

I'll not reply. Let Charlie
choose his own cabana--
in a border adobe or troubled
city project. Perhaps he'll find
a fun-loving amiga--
I hope he took his guitar.

Virginia E. Smith

JUSTICE

The monkey peers out
through the bars having
ceased for a moment
his urgent business of grooming.
He exists in fear of the outer
world, two legged giants
howling in gruff voices.
Though he does not understand
the speech, he recognizes
the contempt in their tones.
Angered, mortified, he swings
    by his tail,
    clutches the bars,
    spits out at the crowd.
    As spectators retreat,
the monkey appeased, continues
grooming, having equated his
    own disdain to
    his ego's satisfaction.

Harry B. Sheftel

THERE ARE MOMENTS

There are moments in our lifetime
When we see with crystal clearness;
There are flashes, call them fire-flames,
When our instincts outweigh reason.
Intuitions or perceptions,
Visions that appear before us
Have as purpose to instruct us.
Conscious as we are of frailties,
We are worried by these flashes.
Though we know these heightened moments
Soon will leave us, will desert us,
These indeed we should remember
These are rare gifts of perception,
When the inner voice directs us.

Lucille D. Short

II.

Sound Drifts

Sound   drifts
through my open window
words in summer
    lifted
from sentences
by the evening breeze
rise   fall
dancing briefly, entwined
then enter my room
to caress me
laughter, whispers
the hushed tones of lovers
in the warmth of the night

Linda Sorensen

MURAL
(George and Wally Krueger)

A painted wall transforms to a mountain
bordering the lake,
a deer drinking from his waterhole,
a stuffed hawk owl perched upon a tree branch
jutting from the wall.
With artists, Indian and white,
George painted chiefs of full eagle headress
with ermine tails,
braves on horseback,
coop stick in hand,
villages of tipis with symbols.

Camp outs at Glacier National Park
in the Rockies adorned the walls
with Two Medicine Lake, Lake Mac Donald,
inspired the creation of the wall mural.

Wally, a taxidermist,
jungled the room
with mounted elk head, cowhides.
I communed with nature in that living room
and wanted to share its poem.

My uncles, German cowboys,
competed against broncho busters and Indians
in the rodeo dressed in ten gallon hats,
boots, fringed shirts.
A ranch of horses, cattle, pigs shared their world.
Love kept Chiquita, the stallion,
with us longer than most horses.

Their drawling Montana cowboy speech
recalled capitivating experiences
of days past.
George was my Grandmother's twin.

Phyllis Southwell

THEIR WOMEN LAUGHED A LOT

They were five old lions
and their women laughed a lot
their manes long since greyed
white-streaked
to now sloping shoulders
once carried on broad-
blue on white pinstriped suits
John Wayne shoulders bursting
into wide-screened viginity
dragging conquests
like sad old saddle blankets
worn by placed saddle
tightly strapped around
frisky
wild unbroken mares
Who gave up wild screams
for knowing laughter.

Deborah Hale Spears

IMPRESSIONISTIC PORTRAIT

GRETA -- The Glamourous One:
Night...beneath void planets where grim fastness
Cloaked was...with the cold;
Yet -- in all that silence Life was breathing --
Living sagas vastly old!
Lights of rich, rare color lined the skyline
Where pale barrens led......
And through all that strangely frozen quiet,
Fragmentary whispers fled;

She, a woman rich in silent beauty,
Northlike...cool...and white...
Still -- with all the knowingness of women,
Slowly smiled......there, in the night.

Lirrel Starling

GOD IS EVER WITH US

If I was the only one in the universe
And everyone else were gone.
I'd still have GOD and His Heavenly Host;
So I couldn't possibly be alone.

GOD and the Angels above in the sky
Has the knowledge and information
The prophets told in their stories
And the Bible is our confirmation.

The death and resurrection of JESUS
Was foretold by the prophets of old.
GOD gave up his only son
As an atonement to save our soul.

JESUS had the last supper with His Disciples
They ate His bread and drank His wine.
It's His blood and body when we do
For a commemoration of Him anytime.

Frances Steele

POLYHYMNIA

Empty
    The fine fair promise
Barren
    The old lusty dream.
Still--
    For awhile
    Viols--
And each Spring the green willow.
Why was I too small?

Jane Sterling

THANKS FOR "SPANISH LEAPING," ROBERT BLY

How long have I submitted to
the anesthetizing of my brain?
Shoveled sweetened pablum--how long
have I swallowed, then spewed it out again?
Seven days and broken nights per week,
such thoughts fester! How long? How long?

Shall I ever charge naked
down strange paper corridors, or skid
on icy panes outstretched across chasms
of pure fire, loose myself in oozing color--
in diffusion of happy accidents, give up
two-stepping to slow static, fling
pubescent conformity away?

Prometheus-like, I strain against restraints,
yet never stole the sacred fire
nor endured death-bird devourings
nor defied any god since my father.

How long shall I lug these chains--these
self-forged, familiar things? I'll tell you:
I have lately glimpsed thoughts and images
fierce enough to hack them off.
As hope gains nerve, I may yet go leaping!

Shirley A. Stevenson

DE PROFUNDIS

Your figure at wire-barred window
etched against last-straw brick
jutting from time's escarpment
where they held you in escrow

It was after the Christmas season
when we escorted you there --
No birds braved the frozen air
unless they had good reason

From an adjacent building
three men emerged as one --
a fourth was waiting within --
the system forewent a gelding

Endures indelibly
the clarity of that cry
which rocked the wintry sky
and cracked the tomb unholy.

Warren Stevenson

INSIDE, WHERE IT REALLY MATTERS

(Age to Youth)

I know you see me withered and gray,
My eyes with their vision blurred;
You think I've forgotten whatever I knew
And your words I've never heard.

But, you see, I'm still just a child
Inside, where it really matters,
And my mind is filled with youthful thoughts
Though the body often clatters.

My body just got older, you know,
While I was busy in life's game
Doing all those important things
And it'll never again be the same.

There were stories and family around
And laughter flowed as I would dream;
There were songs and music at party time
Beneath the light of the moon's beam.

Though what you see be withered and gray,
And the frame less than it used to be,
Inside hopes and dreams still exist
All portraying the reality of me.

Rebekah Stion

MOMENT THE RELATION CHANGED

Lora of the sea,
You died for me.
Two children on the shore,
Who shared their gifts.
While building castles,
We drifted all the way,
Deeper, deeper, deeper,
Until the big waves came.
Laying there still,
You changed, until,
Before my very eyes
You became a lady.
Lora of the sea,
You died for me.
While part of me died too.
We were never the same.
I drove you home a lady,
But not to my home.
Though I called again,
And you called for me,
The salty baptism
Had proven fatal.
Lora of the sea,
You died for me.

Trebor H. Taylor

THE MONKS

The hooded monks pass by
Crowned in their anonymity.

They flow along
In slow silent flutters,

Like rivers of languid butterflies
Draining out of the world

To pour into a sea of solitude.
And as they journey lightward

To grow in grace,
They shimmer like angels

Whose white wings weave the air,
Pair by pair,

And melt the shadows
Lurking in the world

With the bright resurrection sound
Of their windward jubilation.

Lynn M. Terrett

BLACKHOLE HUMANOIDS

Whither goes this world in the
Fleeting Eighties? Will the
Human Dream only be seen as
Withered on the vine of our
Time, killed by miasmic malice?
Or will we not be afraid to
End this decade dedicated to
The search for intelligent life
Here on planet Earth?
And to the conquest of the cold
Unknown distance between us-
That deep dark space where
Mankind's plaintive cry for
Empathy and intimate contact
Is being irretrievably drawn
Into the swirling vortex of
A blackhole of indifference-
Which is speeding into the
Limits of our universe-
Light years away from the
Desires of our being.

Kenneth D. Thomas

I AM THAT I AM

Who do you say that I am, to a restless world that is groaning
and perishing,
In a dark abyss hopelessly groping, ceaselessly grasping for
life's meaning.
Come unto Me, the only Answer, for I am the Way, the Truth
and the Life.
For the struggling world I am perfect Peace; for stumbling
mankind I am the true Light.

Who do you say that I am, to that desperate, discouraged man--
Disappointed by failures, depressed by guilt, defeated by men's
scams.
Listen to Me, the Living Word, for I bring Good News of Faith,
Hope, and Love.
I am your Mountain-mover, your Overcomer, your Strength
from heaven above.

Who do you say that I am, to the troubled man burdened by
cares untold;
Battered by worries, broken by stress, and by fear he is worn.
Cast all your cares on Me, your Burden-bearer, to find Rest
for your weary soul.
I am a very present help in trouble, a Refuge of quiet Rest
from life's raging storms.

Who do you say that I am, to the seeker with hungry heart and
thirsty soul,
Endlessly searching for hidden treasures in a parched and
barren land.
Discover Me, the Christ of Unsearchable Riches, more precious
than silver, more costly than gold.
The Well of Living Water--the Pearl of Great Price, I am.

Who do you say that I am, to that double-minded man of little faith,
Tossed to and fro by every wind of doctrine on the unstable sea of life.
Forever choose Me, the Anchor of the Soul, the Straight and Narrow Way.
I am Faithful and True--the Same yesterday, forever, and today.

Who do you say that I am, to the arrogant, foolish man who claims there is no god,
For whom babbling, boasting, and striving is "right," and to whom sound Wisdom is never a friend.
Receive Me, the Heir of Salvation--the Christ, the Son of the living God.
I am Alpha and Omega: of all things I am the Beginning and the End.

Linda Hand Thompson

WILD SWANS

Wild swans have summoned me
Back from a journey in the land of my kinsmen.
Wearing a purple rose,
I enter the gate
And know the longing in all my body
For the tender beat of white wings.
It had been told me by my kinsmen,
In the darkened hours of unholy night,
That I must retreat from a land I loved.
Strange images came to me:
Of swans, twisted in the trees
And dying;
Of ponds being empty and dry,
And of flesh torn upon a desolate land.
Now swans,are waiting,
White and strong,
Gently shadowed by the trees.
I put my rose upon the water.
Soon it will be day.

Rebecca Thompson

REALIZATION

This agony, in drawn breath that tears
The spirit from ascending stairs,
To the unattainable perfection
Above the mundane,
(Where worms woven through corpses leave the stain
Of death that fells the highest potentate
That robs the riches of their lofty estate)
Breathing this air lifts the red blood
To a singing of the Muse's flood,
Striving to grasp the golden ring on Life's merry go round
That parades in circles in all its fury and its brassy sound,
Yet misses in human frailty,
Constrained by the chains of the Earth's reality.

David L. Transue

THE PREGNANT WORD

Where in the dark recess
lurks the WORD
to light the path
dispel the doubt,
illuminate the truth?

Where in the wilderness of synonyms
hides the WORD
to hit the mark,
achieve the aim,
encapsulate the aggregate?

Where in that encyclopedic mass
awaits the WORD
to avert bewilderment,
remove ambiguities,
abort verbosity?

Where, buried in that thesarus thicket,
lies the WORD, terse-crisp-concise,
that could have said all the above
without the psycholinguistic hyperbolic syndrome
that clutters epigrammatic articulation?

W. I. Throssell

THE STORMY PETREL

We're not on speaking terms
Said the petrel to the whale,
For when I perched upon your back
You flipped that awful tail.

Then

you took a very sudden dive
That left me in mid-air,
But mighty waves your diving made
Drove me to Neptune's lair.

Although

I could have taken wing
I knew it would be fun
To ride those giant waves again
As I had often done.

So

I rode them far into the night
Till the moon shone on the whale,
Then I perched again upon its back
To await that flipping tail.

Tom Troyer

PROLOGUE

Helen descends
in her secret
a black storm
of hair,

to summer fields
of couplet wheat.
She changes sky
over night.

The grain flexes
back against the Earth
before the weather:
the guitar is torn
from my hands,

shatters
on the fieldstones
as it moves away
a nightmare
in the wind.

I do not want
to love her
in all her horrors.

But my cries
are cut like seed
in blades
of her fast wings,

until,
for a moment,
in violent afternoon,
we rhyme.

Robert Blake Truscott

ORANGE AND PINK PALETTE

Orange and pink palette
achieving a Kansas dawn--
horizons beckon.

In the afternoon,
slightly warm yellow high lights
drying prairie grass

Moonlight reflects sky
blue--deeply mysterious--
Stars our only guide.

Thelma H. Urich

WITHIN THE VELVET WOMB OF NIGHT

Within the velvet womb of night
In gently rolling seas that lave the sand,
Phosphorescent flecks make witches' light
And something beckons from the distant dark.
With care, a shoe and then its mate,
And place them high above the fullest tide.
The wanderer strolls the strand; footsteps
Drifting to the lapping wave.
The unseen voice, still suasive leads him on,
And as a tender lover's soft caress
On legs, on, thighs on breast the sea,
With gentle strokes inflames the winsome call.
There in the jet light is the rendezvous;
And there, with sensuous movement and
A langorous converse, tread a courting dance.

From a tiny seedling fear, in innocence,
Before the consummation of the troth
Withdraw; half sorry, half afraid, yet
Turning to the beach with hurried strokes
And wildly agitated heart;
With fright and melancholy mixed,
Flee to the safety of the road along the shore.
Tomorrow, when the day is in the wave
To return and find my shoes.

Howard Van Dine

MADRAS AND MAGGIE

I touch
  thread smooth and thin
My old skirt
  pale, lovely, warp-worn
Visions arise
  thought touched fabric akin
To the madras
  your life, repaired, once torn
Muted yet pure
  the dark and harsh bleed-blend
What remains is
  luminous light soft-shines
Weathered and washed
  gentle friend you help mend
Patterns in lives
  restore, renew designs
Purple pearling
  wisdom-wording, flowing
Promise, plaid-plied
  Maker woven, you give
All seasons attire,
  there bestowing
On the wearer, Grace-given
  a way to live

Patricia Flower Vermillion

PRELUDE

Shadows of naked trees fall on the snow,
leaves no longer hide the sky
which reigns now with austerity.

Dreams of spring burned up in summer heat,
fall was an echo of the flame,
yet, despite winter frost, new dreams are born
and float like songs through emptiness.

Margit Vincenz

WORSHIP

Faith the ethereal essence of our self.
The embodiment of the way we are and do.
We pray, live and work
ever relating to our peers
carefully caringly aiming ever to give
our Loving Maker our humble thanks;
    for the gifts He gives us.
Only when we truly forget the me in us and put You in
then we truly worship.

Hazel B. Wall

ABSTRACT

Amid the circles
the garish planes
the colorful and psychedillic flat shapes
I looked for a meaning.
Attracted to a bright window
Where bloomed an eye,
I confronted it;
quizzical and serious
it stared back at me,
commanding attention.
A picture I might have thought a joke
except for that eye
with its message,
"Do not pass me lightly,--
under my gaze
have you any feeling for the abstract cones,
the squares and parallelograms?"
I would have made a slight judgment
except for the eye that said,
"The truth now,
do you see, do you understand?"

Mary B. Wall

CARVING THE WILDERNESS

Leaves run crab-like.
Lights on tops of poles give shadows
that roll between the leaves. Before and behind
two shadows walk with me.
The human noise is failing.
The frontier is familiar.

I am old.
Scraps of trash catch my eyes.
People are waiting.
Nothing is said.
The human noise is lost.
The frontier is fat and pale.

These walls reach so high
with dirty broken windows
that hold bright pieces of sky
unevenly in the black.
Between the walls the mud is smooth,
packed, polished by constant walking.
All of space is there to be traveled.
Some count their steps, watching.
Some measure the walls with hands at arm's length.

There should be stairs to climb,
pause, turn and look over miles
of trees blue with haze
at the farthest edges
where birth always is.

Patrick W. Wallace

VANCOUVER: EARLY FEBRUARY

The bay lies calm below pale sun
that peeps for moments only
between low clouds that threaten rain,
yet warmly wrap the city
against late winter's cold.

Indolent sloops with gently swelling sails
drift idly in a scarce-felt breeze
between high hungry freighters
that wait to dock and gorge
to holds' content on prairie grain.

The afternoon brings rain. On city hills
the motorcars swish through the splashy streets,
while far below, at one steep road's sea-end,
floats a tall freighter, mist-veiled, magnified
by watery sunlight that has turned
the upper decks to towers of faery gold.

Frances Walsh

BLOCKADE BALLAD

Carronades boom, recoil and boom again
As a frigate dances off Montauk Point
In deadly minuet with a British corvette.
This new War of 1812 pits fresh American
Ship and men against seasoned sailors
Of the British Empire's line.
Carronades boom, recoil and boom again,
Chopping a mizzenmast to bits,
Spraying the scrubbed deck with death,
Fraying the topsails to ribbons where
Midshipmen gaily scrambled but an hour ago,
Their pristine canvas now a wanton tangle.
Carronades boom, recoil and boom again,
A giant's knife to hack away the braces
That fall on redcoats and tangle their frantic haste.
Top gallants droop drunkenly, a gaff drops
And spankers wave like clotheslines.
Flames lick at the captain's feet and
Carronades are still at last.

May Wareberg

LAST PACKETS

Faces floated up on this particular lake,
and few of those who bobbed in their boats
thought much of it, though certainly,
this manner was odd as contrasted to others.
Those bodies which were cast from the shore
were done so with no care of what was up
or down - as the case may have been.
The radio reports received spoke little of fire,
though smoke blocked the sun even more
than before sounds of guns cracked closer.
It wasn't until a woman leaned unexpectedly
over a boat's bow that an eye was seen to open.
She screamed as an arm thrust fast
from the rusted water and drew her down.
Most said she slipped, others opened
their last packets of cocaine and asked
if please, the music ... turn it higher.

Paul Weinman

TO UNCLE JIM

Dear Uncle Jim;

I see you once again at a table
in the back of the tobacco shop.
I sense far away thoughts
back of those dreamy, blue eyes.
What are you remembering?

The cheers, when you were the star
of the school baseball team?
The fear as you piloted the bomber
over the churches of Cologne?
The anticipation on your wedding night?
Perhaps the feel of your new born son in your arms?

Old man, the muscles ached
after a long day on the job.
Are you remembering the warmth of a home,
supper on the stove?

Are you content as you sit there
with that quiet smile?
Nothing to do but pilot checkers
over other old men's kings?

Geneva Werfal

IN LONELY PRAYER

When poets hone their words in tune, refine
each patterned beat till rhythm sparkles fire,
the poem plays rich cadence like a lyre.
They paint a hummingbird in flight, define
a son's enriching birth, with lines design
the markings on a diamondback, inspire
a magic chain of thought and never tire
the listening ear when metered rhymes combine.

Poets protray a widow's pain, give birth
to incidents in time till poems dare
possess and give Creativity's wealth.
Like seasons turning color to the earth,
they write their poems in lonely prayer
till words escape the destiny of death.

Frances Howelle Williams

SEVENTEENTH CENTURY MINIATURE

Not knowing what o'clock it was
And barely caring,
The woman climbed the stairs
Down
As though middle-of-the-night retrieving
Were an everyday occurrence
Which mattered extraordinarily much.

No basement could be so cluttered
As hers was,
To be so well-ordered:
Trunks
And picture frames and cobwebby pottery
Formed a tapestry of time
No one but her would ever touch.

She found it, this time, the thing
She'd gone seeking,
Beneath a wooden hat-rack,
Upright
As the two damning darning needles
Stuck in the ball of twine
That she'd handled so agilely once

Before she'd stumbled
Upstairs
And gone blind.

Tharin Williamson

LOVER

Your love, free and flowing
Like a petal on the wind-
Falls gently on my chest
And lets me sleep.

R. Wilson

WHEN SPRING CALLS

Sunny daffodils marching along the fence
Trees dusted with a hint of green
Forsythia tossing their golden fronds
Snowy apple blossoms fluffing the bluish sky
Robins listening for worms on lawns
  newly painted green
Sharp March breezes sailing the clouds free
I bring up my paint box, rags, and easel
  from the basement
Spring calls

E. Marie Woerner

THERE ARE WORSE THINGS THAN DYING

With evidence his brain had suffered loss,
They filled him full of tubes, needled his veins,
Then sewed and mended, kept him comatose
Long weeks from when his battered body came.

The members of his family, friends at church
Prayed long and hard that God not let him die...
And then he didn't. There he lies. What's worse,
He doesn't know a soul, he doesn't cry.

The medical and doctor bills destroyed
All that was his, all that his family saved.
They say that good intentions were employed
But we know how that road to hell is paved.

Perhaps we don't perceive when asking You
"Thy will be done" implies acceptance too.

Miriam L. Woolfolk

OMEN

A frozen winter holds my world
in icy hands,
and yet...
last night I dreamed of hyacinths.

You brought them, gathered fresh
and damp with dew
They spilled across the table
purple-dark and orchid-pale

You touched my hand, and all the room
was filled with hyacinths
tumbled on the polished floor.

You touched my face--and I awoke
to emptiness.
and yet...
I vow the air still smelled of hyacinths.

Dorothy Williamson Worth

HUMILITY IS ENDLESS
(T.S. Eliot)

After the bitterness
    has made vinegar of your voice
and the last of your friends
    has slammed out the door,

And when the most ancient of wrinkled faces
    has been covered and sealed
following a life of fear
    and self-judgment,

The stars marking the universe
    of your imagination
will aid me as I chart my course
    long after their extinction.

James A. Zoller